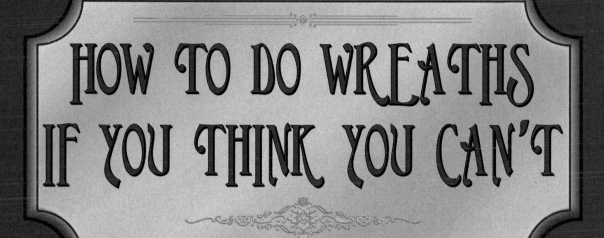

HOW TO DO WREATHS IF YOU THINK YOU CAN'T

The publisher and designers wish to thank the following companies for providing materials used in this publication:

- ❀ **Adhesive Technologies, Inc.** for low temperature glue gun and sticks
- ❀ **Aleene's** for tacky craft glue
- ❀ **American Oak Preserving Co.** for dried and preserved materials, grasses, grapevine and pine cone wreaths
- ❀ **B.B. World Corp.** for mini silk materials
- ❀ **C.M. Offray & Son, Inc.** for ribbon
- ❀ **Design Master color tool, inc.** for wood-tone glossy stains
- ❀ **Fiberex, Inc.** for American Moss® excelsior
- ❀ **Floracraft Corp.** for Styrofoam® products
- ❀ **International Flower Imports, Inc.** for dried and preserved flowers, greenery, pods and foliage wreath bases
- ❀ **Lion Ribbon Co., Inc.** for ribbon, cord and braid
- ❀ **Luzon Imports** for all TWIGS™ items
- ❀ **Modern Forge** for hurricane lamps
- ❀ **MPR Associates, Inc.** for paper lace ribbon
- ❀ **Panacea Products Corp.** for wreath ring forms and floral wire
- ❀ **Schusters Of Texas, Inc.** for raffia, feathers, dried flowers, fruits, pods, cones, and mushrooms
- ❀ **Select Farms, Ltd.** for dried materials, foliage wreath basis and the German statice wreath
- ❀ **Smithers-Oasis USA** for glue pan and pellets and floral foam
- ❀ **Sopp America, Inc.** for ribbon
- ❀ **Teter's Floral Products, Inc.** for silk and latex stems, bushes, pine garlands, wreaths, swags and stems, and Christmas picks
- ❀ **Vaban-Gille** for root wreaths and the abaca witch
- ❀ **Wang's International, Inc.** for silk and latex stems and picks, garlands, vine and root wreaths, Halloween cats, birdhouses, novelty items, plush animals, Santa and birds.
- ❀ **Winward Silks** for silk and latex flowers, berries, fruits and greenery

ABOUT THE DESIGNERS:

Teresa Nelson is the master designer and vice president of Hot Off The Press. She has written more than 50 books on floral design, weddings, appliqué, fabric painting, jewelry making and gift wrapping. Her books have sold over one million copies world-wide. Hot Off The Press is proud to have this very talented lady designing exclusively for us!

Anne-Marie Spencer lives in Oregon with her best friend, Laurence, and is the latest addition to the Hot Off The Press staff. Her background includes creating floral designs for many national catalog publications as well as traveling abroad to design basketware. She is kept very busy at Hot Off The Press, and is already hard at work on two new publications.

Jan Earle began his floral designing career very early, working in his father's floral shop in Colorado. He eventually became an importer and distributor of floral materials. Currently Jan makes his home out in the Oregon countryside.

Reva McCord is retired, but still dabbles in floral arranging when the mood strikes. Her Pod & Cone Wreath on page 131 is a variation of a design she produced and sold for a number of years in the Portland, Oregon area. Reva lives and plays in a small town in Oregon.

PRODUCTION CREDITS:

Project editor: Mary Margaret Hite
Technical editor: LeNae Gerig
Photographer: Meredith Marsh
Graphic designers: Lisa Klupenger, Sally Clarke
Digital imagers: Michael Kincaid, Larry Seith
Editors: Paulette Jarvey, Teresa Nelson, Tom Muir

published by

P.O. Box 55595
Little Rock, Arkansas 72215

produced by

Library of Congress catalog number 96-78533
Hardcover ISBN 0-8487-1578-0
Softcover ISBN 1-57486-060-9

HOW TO DO WREATHS IF YOU THINK YOU CAN'T

TABLE OF CONTENTS

Getting Started

Quick & Easy Wreaths

Vine Wreaths

Wreaths Taken A·P·A·R·T

Straw Wreaths

Twig Wreaths

Styrofoam Wreaths

Christmas Wreaths

Not Your Average, Ordinary Wreath

IDENTIFICATION OF FLORAL MATERIALS

Walking into a floral department in a craft store can be so overwhelming if you aren't prepared for what you'll see or if you're not sure of what you need. Our list of materials needed for each project should help, but what if you don't know the difference between a latex and a silk flower? This section has photos of the most commonly used materials in flower-arranging with a short explanation of their properties. While not every store carries every stem used in the book, knowledge of what you're searching for will help should you need to substitute stems.

Fluff the silk flower, pine or fir stems before using them in a project. Garlands are usually sold coiled, so the sprigs are mashed close to the main stem. Bend the stems and sprigs to curve naturally. If the leaves are wired, shape them to extend among the blossoms or fruit. On pine or fir wreaths, shape each sprig to extend as desired; usually angling them all one direction, either clockwise or counterclockwise around the wreath, provides the most natural look. Grape stems usually have wired tendrils which may be stretched out of shape. Wrap the tendrils around a round pen, remove the pen and slightly stretch the coil for a natural look.

Polysilk Flowers
Because "silk" flowers aren't actually made from silk, but from polyester, they hold their shapes well; some are actually weatherproof. In recent years the quality of polysilks has greatly improved, with more realistic flowers being created. Natural colors are used, with shading or veining in the petals to make them more botanically correct.

"Dried-Silk" Flowers
These are polysilk flowers, but with curled edges which make them look dried.

Delores Ruzicka, a designer in Nebraska, has discovered a method of turning regular polysilks into dried silks which she calls "flower zapping." Hold the flower by the stem in one hand; direct the heat from a heat gun or paint stripper onto the petals and leaves, being very careful not to burn yourself. Begin on a low temperature setting to acquaint yourself with the process.

Zapping stems of polysilk leaves can make them more realistic. Orange, yellow and brown autumn leaves, as well as regular green leaves, once zapped, can become very attractive additions to floral designs.

Hand-Wrapped Flowers

Most elegant silk and parchment flowers are actually hand-wrapped, meaning they're assembled by hand and the stems are wrapped with floral tape. Their stems can be hard to cut, because the flowers and leaves are on separate wire stems which are wrapped together onto a heavier wire.

Of course, the more effort put into producing the flowers, the more expensive they become. However, a design using high-quality, realistic flowers can be enjoyed much longer than the inexpensive polysilks; they will be in style longer with their colors spanning more seasons.

Foam Flowers:

Brand new on the scene are foam flowers, constructed of high-density, very thin foam. Usually, as is the case with the flowers shown, the leaves or thicker parts of the flowers are foam with the blossom being polysilk. The results are blossoms and leaves which are extremely realistic to view and to touch.

In an effort to make silk flowers more botanically correct and to add visual interest to arrangements, manufacturers are now creating flowers with bulbs and roots attached. The only limitation to using these is they must be left intact, making it difficult to achieve varying heights in the design. While being wonderful to use, they also add another level of realism.

Fabric Flowers:

Non-woven fabric is used to make these flowers. It is cut and shaped into petals, which are then hand-wrapped together. The leaves usually include wires to shape them, and flower petals are shaded for more realism. Veins and ridges pressed into the petals as well as muted colors achieved in the finishing process result in a very upscale look.

Latex Flowers

Parchment and silk flowers that have a cool, rubbery feel have been dipped in latex. They're realistic to touch and add an elegant look to an arrangement.

Keep latex flowers from becoming overheated as the latex can soften and become sticky. Store in a cool, dry place.

Silk Bushes

These are available in many configurations, as flowering plants or as greenery with varying numbers of branches attached to one main stem. The branches may vary in length on one stem, making the bush look realistic. Some bushes include more than one type of flower or plant. These are fun to work with, since the colors are already coordinated for you—plus they may be less expensive to use than individual stems! Of course the more branches on a plant stem, the more expensive it becomes. And with more branches to work with, a fuller, lusher design can be made. To use a bush, either insert it as a plant in a design, or cut the branches off the main stem and insert individually. Sprigs may also be cut off each branch and attached to a base.

Flowering Vines & Garlands

Different types of flowers and plants come as long vines. They vary in lengths from 30" to 9 feet and are convenient if a long garland is required.

Garlands can be a base for other materials such as dried or silk flowers, allowing the creation of some unique vines. Dip the flower stem ends in hot glue and insert them among the garland leaves or flowers, making sure they are glued to the main stem. Or wire stems to a long floral garland, end to end.

Pine or Fir Garlands

PVC or vinyl garlands commonly come in 9-foot lengths and are very versatile. They can be cut into shorter lengths and wired to baskets, wreaths or other bases.

It can be quicker and easier to use a garland rather than individual pine stems for designing. A pine garland wired to a grapevine wreath is a great start for a Christmas design. Or, if pine stems are needed but none are on hand, make them by cutting 8–12-sprig sections of pine garland and wiring each to a long wood pick.

To cut a garland, spread apart the individual sprigs and cut through the heavy binding wires; twist the cut wire ends together to secure the sprigs nearest the ends.

Picks

Floral picks are short stems of clustered items. Christmas picks, the most common, may include berries, cones, silk leaves, packages, ornaments, pine sprigs, etc. Short (4"–7" tall) stems of flowers or greenery are also called picks; they are very inexpensive. Flower picks generally include 1–3 blossoms with several leaves per stem. Greenery picks can be small plants, such as violets, or just leaves on a stem; these look especially nice clustered in a design.

While picks can be effective inserted as stems, they can also be cut into individual components. Attach each to a wood pick, then insert into the design in a scattered pattern.

Artificial Fruits & Vegetables

Important elements in floral designing, these are available in polysilk, vinyl, or latex, and can be attached directly to the design, among the materials. If a pick or stem is needed on the fruit or vegetable for insertion into foam, glue one to the bottom or to a hidden area of the piece.

Berries Stems

Stems of berries, whether smooth or textured (like blackberries) have remained popular, adding interest or becoming fillers in a design. More intricate berries with vines and branches are also available. They can look good enough to eat and add color, shine, and unique textures to arrangements.

Berries are available as picks, on stems or as vines. They come with or without leaves and can even be found mixed in with flowers or greenery on the same stem. Berries are fun to include in woodsy designs, adding a wild, natural look.

Pods & Mushrooms

It's easy to find many varieties of pods with a wide range of sizes, colors and textures. Dried tree fungus, also known as dried sponge mushrooms, are a realistic addition to the woodsy, natural look. Mushrooms and pods come attached to wired stems or wood picks, making them easy to use.

canella

eskira pod

bell cup

jacaranda pod

okra pod

sponge mushroom

Cones

Different types of cones are available for purchase, many with heavy stems attached (some have even been cut apart to resemble flowers). Or you can collect your own cones to use in projects.

Always use fresh cones; if they crumble in your hands, they are too old. If they've been collected from trees, rinse them under running water to remove dust and debris, then bake on a cookie sheet at 225° for one hour to open the petals again. Cones can be glued, wired or inserted directly into a project, depending on the look wanted and how they are prepared.

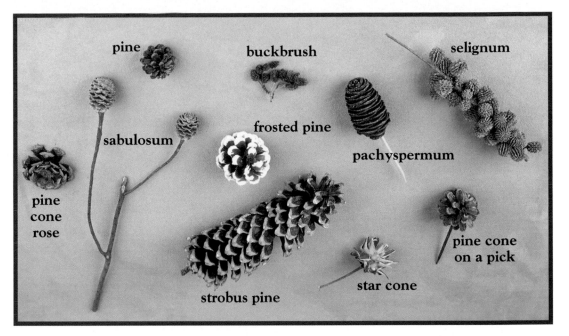

Mosses

Mosses are most often used to cover the mechanics of an arrangement, such as foam, wire or glue. The moss in a design is chosen for its color or texture and is secured with U-shaped floral pins or glue.

Natural Spanish moss is gray; if a soft, neutral look is desired, it works nicely. A product called gray American Moss® imitates Spanish moss but is actually excelsior; it's cleaner to use, with nearly the same effect. Other colors are available in American Moss®, such as green and brown, which can be useful when you want it to show in the design.

Sphagnum moss, also known as sheet moss, is used when a green "growing" look is needed. It comes packaged in layers or in sheets to be peeled apart as needed. Reindeer moss is gray with a unique texture that looks great when it can be seen as part of the design. It's available dried or preserved; the dried version is very brittle, whereas the preserved moss is softer. Mood moss is a very thick green moss and is effectively used in designs where the moss is visible as an important component. It has depth, is firm and is easy to work with, especially on larger projects.

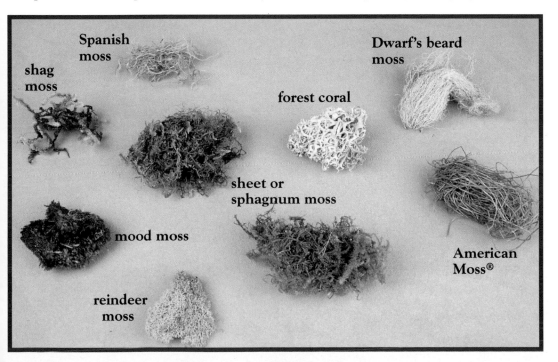

Other more unusual mosses and lichens are available to use in floral design, including forest coral, dwarf's beard and shag moss. All have unique properties and appearances, yet, if one is unavailable, any moss or lichen of similar color and texture can be used in the designs as a substitute. All enhance the natural look and feeling of a design, giving each a "back-to nature" appearance.

abaca fiber

amaranthus

baby everlasting

baby's breath

barley

bell reed

bloom broom

bell cup

lotus pod

avena

linum

lino grass

lepidium

leatherleaf fern

IDENTIFICATION OF DRIED MATERIALS

The dried materials available in stores today include flowers, twigs, branches, grasses, leaves, pods, vegetables and fruits. Rich with textures, these materials are important additions to most floral designs. Dried grasses and pods provide a natural, garden or woodsy look to designs while baby's breath, caspia and German statice are great filler flowers, eliminating empty spaces within arrangements.

Often silk arrangements need the addition of dried materials to make them look more realistic. Most pieces in this book have drieds as part of the design and these pages are provided as an identification guide for the dried materials used. They are placed in alphabetical order, beginning at the upper left and rotating clockwise around these two pages, then continuing in the same manner on pages 14–15.

Flowers and plants can be air-dried naturally, kiln-dried (which preserves more of the color), freeze-dried or processed with a desiccant such as silica gel. Glycerin-preserved materials can be recognized by their fresher feel, softness and pliability.

Before removing very delicate dried materials from their cellophane wrapping, hold the bunch over steam for a minute (be careful the steam

heather

kiwi vine

isolepsis grass

holly oak

lavender

hill flowers

larkspur

hydrangea

jacaranda pod

brisa
maxima

brisa
media

buckbrush
cones

bupleurum

canella

boxwood

bromus
secalinus

caspia

cedar

oesn't burn you). This will soften the flowers and stems a
it, allowing them to be pulled apart more easily without
hattering. A light steaming can also enhance the appear-
nce of many dried flowers, fluffing and refreshing leaves,
lossoms and buds.

f the stems of dried flowers and grasses bend or break
vhen they are inserted into foam, wire wood picks to the
tem bottoms—be sure to insert the picks far enough into
he foam so just the flower stem shows.

Properly cared for, dried arrangements are very long-
asting. Display them out of direct sunlight, which will
ade the blooms. A too-humid environment will cause
he materials to droop, but insufficient humidity or
ligh temperatures will make them brittle and fragile.

Dried plant materials are a pleasure to work with and
an make an ordinary floral design extraordinary.

christina grass

cinnamon sticks

eskira
pod

floral buttons

pheasant
feathers

willow
eucalyptus

spiral
eucalyptus

Frasier fir

fiber
ball
pod

excelsior

ming fern

forest coral

ming moss

sphagnum moss

shag moss

mehogni pod

dwarf's beard

sheet moss

reindeer moss

Spanish moss

starflowers

Siberian statice

statice sinuata

stirlingia

star cones

German statice

statice suworowii

spruce

sprengeri

sabulosum cones

safflower

sponge mushroom

salal

roses

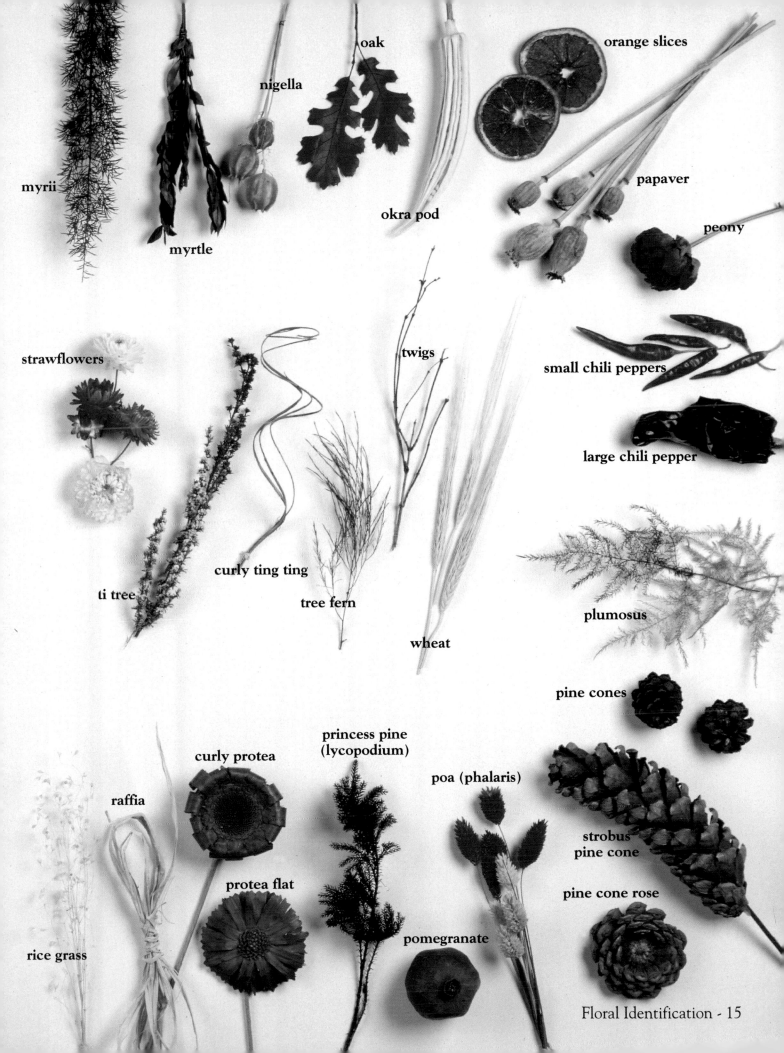

myrii

nigella

oak

orange slices

myrtle

papaver

okra pod

peony

strawflowers

twigs

small chili peppers

large chili pepper

curly ting ting

ti tree

tree fern

plumosus

wheat

pine cones

princess pine
(lycopodium)

curly protea

poa (phalaris)

raffia

strobus
pine cone

protea flat

pine cone rose

pomegranate

rice grass

SUBSTITUTION OF MATERIALS

We make every effort to use widely distributed floral materials in our designs. But, with more than 100,000 new items introduced every year, it can sometimes be difficult to find all the exact materials required for any one project. With a little creativity, it's an easy task to substitute other flowers for ones listed.

When substituting, find flowers that are similar to those listed in the project. Check to make sure each is approximately the size required with as many blossoms as needed. If you're substituting a different type of flower, make sure it's the same shape: A 3" wide rose or carnation might be substituted for a 3" wide mum. The texture will be a little different, but the design shouldn't suffer for it.

Sometimes it may be difficult to find just the exact Christmas pick described in the text of a project. In this case, the colors and "look" of the pick used become more important than exactly what is in it. If the project is to be woodsy or have a natural look, then the pick needs to have that same look in the desired colors.

Substituting dried materials when the correct type can't be found is also easy. If you're looking for a certain cone or pod, any cone or pod of similar size and color could replace the original. If several styles of pods are needed to complete a project, it's probably important that different pods are used, but maybe not those exact ones. (If the same pod is used throughout, the design might become boring; different styles of pods add texture and interest to a piece.)

If a certain dried flower or grass in unavailable, look at that material in the photo and try to find one which is similar. For instance, fillers such as gypsophila, rice grass, baby's breath and caspia can easily substitute for each other because they have similar characteristics, with fine flowers or seeds which will extend equally well among the larger components of the arrangement. If the product is bulky or heavy, substitute a product of similar weight.

Many times silk flowers can replace dried ones in an arrangement, too. Silk baby's breath comes in different colors and is easy to add into an arrangement which originally calls for dried baby's breath. There are many latex fruits, pods and vegetables which are great substitutes for similar dried materials. The advantage to using silk and latex pieces in place of dried materials is their longevity. They don't shatter like dried flowers, allowing the arrangement to remain beautiful longer.

It's a little more difficult to substitute dried flowers for silk. Generally, air-dried blossoms are smaller, thus harder to use as a large focal point in a design. Not every polysilk is available as a dried flower, so substituting other flower types may be necessary when converting a silk arrangement to drieds.

If colors need to be changed to match your decor, determine the dominant color in the design and choose the number of flowers listed in the desired color. Repeat through the list, substituting your chosen colors for the ones listed. When you've gathered all the flowers, hold them together in a bunch to make sure the new colors blend well. If there's a ribbon in the design, hold it with the flowers to be sure everything coordinates.

Substituting can be an exciting adventure in creativity! Be patient and play with the colors, sizes and textures to make sure they will blend well and produce the look and feeling desired.

Some wreath bases are so pretty it's almost a shame to add materials which cover them. A crescent design solves that dilemma. It's a floral design formed in a curved shape on a portion of the wreath, leaving the remainder of the base uncovered. As a result, the exposed vines, sprigs, roots or twigs add texture and charm to the entire design.

Shown here are four variations of the crescent design. The two wreaths above feature crescents angled on the lower areas of the bases. The exposed whitewashed and lacquered vines become important elements within the designs and reinforce the styles.

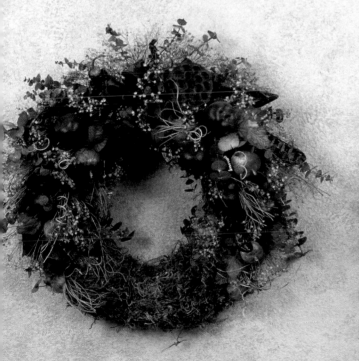

Here are two more examples, these with the crescents created on the upper and lower portions of the bases. The wreath on the left features an elongated crescent extending quite far down each side. To balance the weightiness of the poinsettias in the lower crescent on the Christmas wreath, a smaller, secondary focal has been added at the top.

Crescents are simple to create and economical when using some of the more expensive latex and silk materials. When creating your crescent design, first try moving your components around the wreath base; maybe shifting the crescent to a new location allows the finished piece to fit in more naturally with its surroundings.

Tools, Supplies & Putting It All Together

The following pages include explanations and photos of all kinds of floral tools and supplies. Sometimes it's difficult to know just which supplies are really needed to complete a project; this information should clear up some of the confusion and make it easier to decide what is needed and when. There are some tips for using certain supplies, too.

knife   scissors   pliers   wire cutters

Tools

A sharp serrated knife, scissors, needle-nose pliers, and heavy-duty wire cutters are valuable tools in dried and silk floral work. The wire cutters need to be sturdy enough to cut through the heavy stems of hand-wrapped silks. Use the pliers to twist wires together, saving tender hands and fingernails. The knife is used to trim floral foam to fit a base. Scissors should be sharp enough to cut ribbons, and shouldn't be used to cut wire, which will nick and dull the blades.

Wires

(A) Wires are measured by gauge—the smaller the number, the heavier the wire. 18–20 gauge wire is used to lengthen or strengthen flower stems (see "Floral Tape," page 14). 22–24 gauge wire is a nice weight for bows or loop hangers. 30-gauge wire is very fine and can be used to attach stems to bases and to secure ribbon loops. **(B)** Paddle wire is fine- to medium-weight wire rolled onto a wooden paddle and is used whenever a continuous length is needed.

(C) Cloth-covered wires come in either green or white. Green wires resemble flower stems and blend in well with designs. The white wire is useful when doing bridal work. Both are available in stem weight as well as lighter weights for securing items together.

(D) Chenille stems can be used instead of wire to secure bows. Because of their fuzziness, they don't slip as easily—and because of their wide range of colors, it's easy to match them to your ribbon.

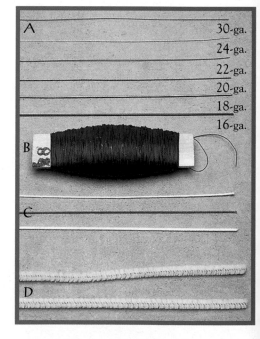

A — 30-ga.
24-ga.
22-ga.
20-ga.
18-ga.
16-ga.
B
C
D

Making a Wire Loop or U-Pin Hanger

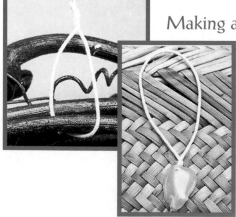

First decide the best placement for a hanger so the project hangs correctly (some projects, such as a heart-shaped wreath, will require more than one hanger). Insert a 6"–10" length of 24-gauge wire into the back (such as among the vines of a wreath). Bring the end back out and twist both ends together, forming a loop. If the object is solid and a wire can't be inserted, make a wire loop first and hot glue it to the back. (White wire was used here for visibility.)

An easy hanger for a straw or foam wreath can be made by bending the ends of a U-shaped floral pin back and inserting them into the wreath. For extra strength, secure the U-pin with hot glue.

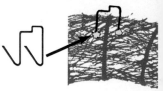

Glues

Tacky craft glue effectively secures stems in floral foam. Dip the cut stem into glue, then insert it into the project. Gluing keeps stems from twisting in or dislodging from the foam, ruining established design lines.

Hot or low temperature glue guns are handy for floral designing. The low temperature gun is safer, but not as secure as hot glue when used on items preserved with glycerine. Apply glue to the stem end, then insert it into foam or onto the base. Hold the item for a moment until the glue sets. Glue sticks are available in different formulas; make sure you use the correct stick for the job and the gun.

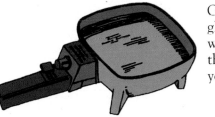

Glue pans, which hold a pool of melted glue at a constant temperature, are useful when you have a lot of gluing to do, since they let you keep one hand free by allowing you to dip the stems.

Floral Foam

Floral foam is available in two types: fresh or "wet" foam and dry foam. Wet foam should be used only for fresh flowers. Because it is made to soak up water and hold it for the fresh stems, it's too soft for dried and silk arrangements. Dry foam, designed to be used with silk and dried flowers, is firmer and holds stems more securely.

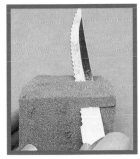

To prepare dry foam prior to attaching it to a base, use a serrated knife to cut it to size—trim away as much as possible, leaving a smaller area to be concealed. Cut the corners down to make it fit; if placed in a container, trim it to match the container with 1" extending above the rim. If the foam is to fit into a wreath, be sure to trim away enough so the foam fits snugly against the inner side.

Use the knife to round the top edges and corners of the foam. This will make it easier to cover with moss or excelsior and make the "ground" where the stems are inserted look more natural. Do not cut away so much of the foam that it no longer extends the correct amount above the rim of the container. It's much easier to achieve a natural, growing look in an arrangement if you're able to insert stems into the foam sides parallel with the table. Usually no more than 1" needs to extend above the rim to achieve this effect.

To attach floral foam to a base, glue or wire it in place. To wire it, first cover an area on the top of the foam with a strip of moss or excelsior, then wrap a 30-gauge wire length over the foam and around the base, twisting the ends at the back to secure. The moss prevents the wire from pulling through the foam.

A

B

C

Wood Picks

These add length or strength to floral items. To add a wired wood pick to a cluster of dried flowers:

(A) position the flowers in the cluster at varying heights, then cut the stems in the same place.

(B) Place the stems against the pick; wrap the wire around both the pick and the stems.

(C) Continue wrapping down the pick for 1", then wrap back up the stems, using all the wire.

Wood picks also come without wires. These can be floral-taped to stems or glued to the backs of stemless items such as pods, charms and novelties.

U-Shaped Floral Pins

Also called "greening pins," these are used to pin moss, ribbon loops, or other items into foam. If the item being secured has a tendency to spring out of the foam, apply a dab of glue to the pin ends before inserting. These can be used as hangers for Styrofoam® and straw wreaths (see page 18).

A

B

Floral Tape

This is a paper tape which has a waxy coating; stretching the tape as it's being wrapped makes it to stick to itself. Use floral tape to secure wire or a pick to a flower stem, lengthening or reinforcing it (also called "stemming a flower").

(A) Place a length of 18-gauge wire next to the stem of a flower.

(B) Wrap the stem and the wire together with floral tape, gently stretching the tape so it adheres to itself. Tape to the end of the wire.

Measuring & Cutting Floral Stems

A "stem" refers to the entire stem of flowers as purchased. When cut apart, the pieces are called "sprigs" or "branches."

When a blossom width is given, measure the open flower head.

When a blossom height is given, measure only the blossom.

When a stem length is given, measure only the stem.

When a flower length is given, measure from the top of the blossom to the end of the stem.

Unless otherwise specified, flower measurements given within a project include 1½"–2" of stem to be inserted into the design. By cutting the stems with extra length, you are able to adjust the height of the flower within the arrangement, playing with it until it's exactly right. Using tacky craft glue to secure stems lets you, while the glue is still wet, pull out a stem that is too long, trim and reinsert it without destroying the foam. If a stem is too short, lengthen it with a stem wire (see "Floral Tape," page 14), then cut to the correct length.

Wiring a Cone

To wire a cone so it can be attached to a base:

A

(A) Use a 10" length of 24-gauge wire. Measure 3" from one end and insert the wire between two rows of cone petals near the bottom.

B

(B) Wrap the wire around the cone, pulling tightly, then twist the wire ends so they extend from the cone. Use these wire ends to attach the cone to the project. For another look, wrap the wire among the upper petals so the bottom of the cone will show in the project.

Three Ways to Attach a Pick or Stem to a Pod or Cone

(A) Drill a hole into the bottom. Fill the hole with glue and insert the blunt end of an unwired wood pick into the hole.

(B) Wrap the wire of a wood pick around the cone petals, pulling it down inside the cone. Wrap completely around the cone, using all the wire.

(C) Hot glue a U-shaped floral pin to the cone bottom.

A

B

C

RIBBONS & BOWS

Some people think one of the most difficult tasks in making a floral project is making the bow. Not so!

The easiest way to learn is to buy a reel of inexpensive acetate ribbon—enough so you don't feel guilty using as much as you want—and practice making bows. The freedom of knowing you can use as much as you want until you get it down makes learning much easier than if you use the expensive tapestry ribbon you bought just for a certain project. Eventually, making bows will become second nature (and you'll be asked by everyone in your house, office or neighborhood to please make this one bow for little Jennifer's birthday gift . . .well, you get the picture). Of course, you could offer to teach a class on bow-making to all those friends, family members and neighbors.

We've included instructions, photos and illustrations of the bows used in this book. Generally, if you choose a narrower ribbon than the one suggested, you will need more of it—and to make more loops—to make sure the bow has the same impact within the design. Likewise, if a wider ribbon is chosen, you'll probably want fewer loops to make sure the bow doesn't overpower the project.

Ribbons and bows are beautiful additions to florals, but the styles of ribbons available are almost endless, and it can be confusing to choose just the right pattern for a project. However, you'll find that the flower colors and the style of the arrangement will narrow your choices.

Ribbon Styles

Ribbons are available with different edge treatments; this can be important in design, as some edges will fray with frequent handling. *Woven edge ribbon* has a finished edge which will not fray. This ribbon is easy to use in bows because of its softness and pliability.

Picot ribbon is a woven edge ribbon distinguished by small loops extending outward from each edge. Including picot ribbon with plain ribbons in a multi-ribbon bow adds texture and interest. Picot ribbons add a nice touch to romantic designs.

Wire-edged ribbon is easy to use because it has "memory"; each edge is woven around a thin wire. If a bow becomes crushed it's easy to reshape the loops, making the bow look new. The tails can be rippled and tucked among design components, with the wires holding the shape. The wires can be pulled to easily shirr the ribbon.

Cut edge ribbons are often used in floral work. Less expensive, they are available in many of the same patterns and designs as woven or wire-edged ribbon. To reduce fraying, sizing is added—this stiffens the ribbon, but also means that any creases made in forming the bow will remain visible. Eventually the edges will fray, so handle the ribbon as little as possible.

Paper ribbon has become a floral design staple. Some of these ribbons come twisted into cords and can be used that way, or untwisted to make crinkly flat ribbon. The twisted cords make fun accents twined through and around a bow made from flat paper ribbon. Printed paper ribbons are marketed both on reels or in packaged lengths. Their patterns are muted, making them nice for dried arrangements. Also available are lacy paper ribbons with cut-out areas resembling eyelet.

Choosing Your Ribbons:

The ribbons you use can determine the entire look of your design. For example, heavy tapestries give a more European look, while narrow satin ribbons add a light, romantic effect. The ribbon should tie the design together and actually become part of it.

In choosing a ribbon, both color and width play important roles. Incompatible colors or textures can produce a jarring effect. Using a ribbon which has all the colors in the design—or nearly all of them—ties the design together.

If one ribbon with the right colors can't be found, use two or three ribbons, each in one of the colors needed, and stack the bows. Make a large bow of the widest ribbon (usually the dominant color in the design), then wire or glue a smaller bow of narrower ribbon to the center of it.

Another method of tying colors together is to make one bow of several different ribbons. Hold them together and handle as if they were one length to make a bow of the desired size and type.

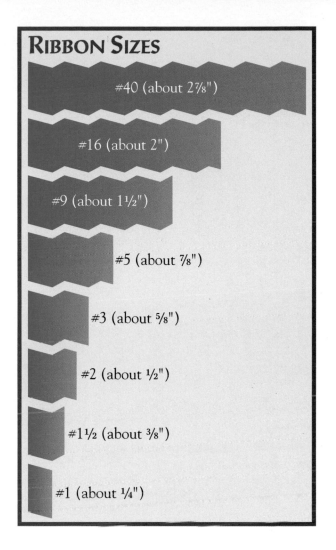

RIBBON SIZES

#40 (about 2⅞")

#16 (about 2")

#9 (about 1½")

#5 (about ⅞")

#3 (about ⅝")

#2 (about ½")

#1½ (about ⅜")

#1 (about ¼")

HOW MUCH DO I NEED?

Although projects in this book include the yardage needed for each bow in the materials list, you may want to make a different bow. First decide how many loops and tails you want, and how long they will be (if you want a center loop, double its length, add ½" and add this measurement along with the tails.) Then do this easy math:

1. ____" (loop length) x 2 + ½" extra (for the twist) = A

2. A x (number of loops) = B

3. B + ____" (tail length) + ____" (tail length) = C

4. C ÷ 36" = yardage required.

FOR EXAMPLE:

To make a bow with eight 4" loops, a 6" tail and a 7" tail,

1. 4" x 2" + ½" = 8½"

2. 8½" x 8 loops = 68"

3. 68" + 6" (tail length) +7" (tail length) = 81"

4. 81" ÷ 36" = 2.25 or 2¼ yards.

Many times ribbon is used to bring different design elements together visually. This is done by tucking, rippling or looping ribbon lengths or the bow tails among the other materials in the project. Twisting the ribbon as it's looped adds interest. If the base is visible in one area of the design (such as on a vine wreath with all the flowers at the upper left), wrapping the ribbon around the bare areas will help tie the design together. The ribbon draws your eye into the undecorated space.

Other materials such as cord, braid, pearls, beads or wired star garlands can be used with or in place of ribbon.

For wide ribbons a "couched" effect can be achieved by pinching the ribbon every few inches and wrapping the pinched areas with 30-gauge wire. The ribbon will puff between the wires. Glue the wired areas into the design.

Shoestring Bow

1 Measure the desired tail length from the end of the ribbon, then make a loop of the specified length. Wrap the free end of the ribbon loosely around the center of the bow.

2 Form a loop in the free end of the ribbon and push it through the center loop. Pull the loops in opposite directions to tighten, then pull on the tails to adjust the size of the loops. Trim each tail diagonally or in an inverted V.

Collar Bow

1 Form a ribbon length into a circle, crossing the ends in front. Pinch together, forming a bow, and adjust the loop size and tail length. If no tails are desired, form the length into a circle and just barely overlap the ends before pinching into a bow.

2 Wrap the center with wire and twist tightly at the back to secure. Trim the wire ends, then wrap a short length of ribbon over the center wire and glue the ends at the back. Cut each tail diagonally or in an inverted V.

Raffia Collar Bow:

Hold 20–30 raffia strands together and form them into a circle, crossing the ends at the bottom. Pinch together, forming a bow, and adjust the loop sizes and tail lengths. Tie the center with a raffia strand; knot it at the back. Blend the ends into the other tails.

Standup Bow

Measure the desired tail length and hold the ribbon. Make a loop, positioning it to extend upward beside the tail. Repeat to make as many loops as desired. Fold a tail up to match the first tail, then trim the ribbon. Wrap wire tightly around the bottom of the loops to secure.

Flat Bow

1 Begin with one end of the ribbon and make a center loop the desired length. Twist the ribbon to keep the right side showing.

2 Make a loop the specified length on one side of your thumb. Twist the ribbon and form a matching loop on the other side.

3 Continue making loops of graduating sizes on each side of your thumb, positioning each just under the last loop, until the desired number is reached. For the tails, bring the ribbon end up and hold in place under the bow.

4 Insert a wire length through the center loop. Bring the ends to the back, catching the ribbon end, and twist to secure. Cut the ribbon tails to the desired lengths, then trim each tail diagonally or in an inverted V.

Oblong Bow

1 Form a center loop by wrapping the ribbon around your thumb. Twist the ribbon a half turn to keep the right side showing, then make a loop on one side of the center loop.

2 Make another half twist and another loop on the other side. Make another half twist and form a slightly longer loop on each side of your hand; notice these loops are placed diagonally to the first loops.

3 Make two more twists and loops on the opposite diagonal. Continue for the desired number of loops, making each set slightly longer than the previous set.

4 **For tails:** Bring the ribbon end up and hold in place under the bow. Insert a wire through the center loop, bring the ends to the back of the bow, and twist tightly to secure. Trim each tail diagonally or in an inverted V.

Puffy Bow

1 If a center loop is required, begin with one end of the ribbon length and make the center loop. Twist the ribbon to keep the right side showing. If no center loop is called for, begin with step 2.

2 Make a loop on one side of your thumb. Give the ribbon a twist and make another loop, the same length as the first, on the other side of your thumb. Continue making loops and twists until the desired number is reached (a ten-loop bow has five loops on each side), ending with a twist.

3 **For tails:** Bring the ribbon end up and hold in place under the bow, making a long loop (two or more loops can be made for multiple tails). Insert a wire through the center loop, bring the ends to the back of the bow, and twist tightly to secure. Trim each tail diagonally or in an inverted V.

Loopy Bow

1 Measure the desired tail length from the end of the ribbon and make a loop on each side of your thumb. If a center loop is needed, measure the desired tail length from the end of the ribbon and make the center loop before the bow loops.

2 Continue making loops on each side of your thumb until the desired number is reached (for a ten-loop bow, make five loops on each side).

3 Wrap the center with wire and twist tightly at the back to secure. If a center loop was made, insert the wire through it before twisting the ends at the back. Trim the wire ends. Cut each tail diagonally. Or secure the bow by wrapping a length of ribbon around the center and tying it at the back—this adds a second set of tails.

Loopy Bow with Center Loop

Raffia Loopy Bow:

1 Measure the desired tail length from one end of a raffia strand, then make a loop on each side of your thumb.

2 Continue to loop the raffia strand back and forth until all the raffia is used but enough for the opposite tail. Wire to secure, or tie the center with another strand of raffia and knot it at the back to secure. (If a fuller bow is desired, repeat with another strand before securing.)

Raffia Loop:

Hold the specified number of strands together. Measure the desired tail length from one end and hold the strands together at that point. Fold the strands above your hand, making a loop of the specified length, and repeat until all the raffia is used. Wire at the base of the loop, turning the tails upward or letting them hang, as indicated in the project.

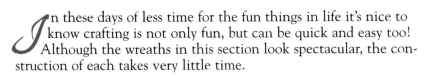

Quick & Easy Wreaths

*I*n these days of less time for the fun things in life it's nice to know crafting is not only fun, but can be quick and easy too! Although the wreaths in this section look spectacular, the construction of each takes very little time.

Three of the featured designs begin with an "almost-finished" wreath base. Silk and dried floral materials are added to complete them, turning each into a beautiful wreath ready to be hung on a door to greet guests or on a wall as a permanent decoration.

Many craft stores carry dried wreaths which are pretty alone, but sometimes look unfinished. We've used these to show what can be accomplished with just the addition of a few stems and a bow. Because all the time-consuming construction has been done by the manufacturer, these wreaths become very quick and easy to complete.

Should you decide you want to create your own base, the Eucalyptus & Evergreen Wreath on page 31 shows the quickest method for doing so. The metal ring with prongs makes assembling the wreath just a matter of cutting the sprigs, holding them together and bending the prongs over the stems. A rich and stylish look is accomplished that quickly!

Many of the other projects in this section consist of crescent designs on wreaths. Because the crescent covers just a portion of the wreath, the completion of the design is faster than covering the entire wreath base. This allows the vines of the base to become part of the design, adding texture and interest.

Whichever designs you decide to create, we've done our best to make some wonderful designs which also happen to be fast. Have fun creating these quick and easy wreaths—and for a customized look, try adding some materials we didn't think to use!

Fuchsia Heart

24" wide TWIGS™ heart wreath
2 stems of bright mauve silk fuchsias,
    each with two 3" blossoms, two 2"
    blossoms, 2 buds and many leaves
2 stems of dusty burgundy artificial
    cranberries, each with four 7" sprigs
    of five ¾" berries and 2 leaves
1 stem of fuchsia/white silk baby's
    breath, each with three 9" sprigs
    with 5 clusters of three ¾" blooms
3¾ yards of 1½" wide fuchsia/brown
    printed fabric ribbon
1 oz. of dried burgundy christina grass
1 oz. of preserved baby's breath
24-gauge wire
low temperature glue gun and sticks

1 Bend the fuchsia stems to follow the wreath curves and wire one on each side, placing the first blossom at the wreath top as shown. Trim the excess stem. Repeat with a berry stem on each side.

2 Use the ribbon to make a puffy bow (see page 26) with a center loop, ten 3" loops, two 14" tails and two 20" tails. Wire to the center top of the heart. Let the 14" tails drape through the heart center; tuck and glue a 20" tail among the flowers and berries on each side. Cut the christina grass heads into 3"–4" sprigs. Glue evenly spaced among the berries and flowers throughout wreath and bow loops, following the lines of the wreath twigs.

3 Cut the silk baby's breath clusters to 1½"–2". Glue evenly spaced among the flowers and bow loops.

4 Cut the preserved baby's breath into 2"–3" sprigs. Glue evenly spaced among the flowers and bow loops. Make a wire loop hanger (see page 18) at the center back.

Eucalyptus & Evergreen Wreath

10" wide wreath ring with prongs
6 oz. of green preserved eucalyptus
6 oz. of green preserved cedar
6 oz. of green preserved wild boxwood
6 oz. of green preserved Frazier fir
4 oz. of dark pink preserved heather
2 oz. of white preserved statice sinuata
1 stem of burgundy artificial berries
    with 7 sprigs of five ⅜" wide berries
9 sabulosum cones
24-gauge wire
low temperature glue gun and sticks

wreath ring

1 Cut all the preserved materials except the cones into 6"–9" sprigs; divide into ten equal bunches (or make one bunch for each pair of prongs on your wreath ring). Hold the stems of one bunch together, shorter stems on top, with the stem ends even. Fan the bunch to 5" wide and lay it between one pair of prongs with the stems extending 1"–1½" beyond the prongs. Fold the prongs securely over the stems.

2 Repeat the process nine times. For the last bunch, bend the first bunch upward, exposing the last pair of prongs, and insert the stems; secure.

3 Cut the berry stem into seven 4" sprigs. Referring to the large photo, glue the sprigs evenly spaced throughout the wreath. Glue the cones as shown in the large photo. Make a wire loop hanger (see page 18) on the upper back.

Cherry Blossoms & Lavender

14" round dried German
  statice wreath
1 stem of pink silk
  cherry blossoms with 11
  sprigs of ¾"–1½" flower
  clusters and buds
1 stem of dusty green silk ivy
  with three 16" sprigs of
  many 1½"–2½" wide
  leaves
2 stems of mauve silk roses,
  each with four 1½"–2" wide
  blossoms and 2 buds
1 stem of mauve artificial
  berries with seven 4" long
  sprigs of five ⅜" wide berries
1 stem of mauve dried-silk larkspur with many ¾"–1½"
  wide blossoms
1½ oz. of dried lavender
2 yards of 1⅜" wide white lace
  ribbon
24-gauge wire
low temperature glue gun and
  sticks

1 Cut the ivy sprigs off the stem; set one aside for step 3. Wire the others stem to tip around the wreath front, leaving 4"–5" open at 10:00.

2 Cut each cherry blossom cluster and bud with a 1" stem. Glue the blossoms evenly spaced among the ivy leaves; fill in any empty spaces with the buds.

3 Cut each rose and bud with a 1" stem; set the buds aside for step 4. Glue the roses evenly spaced among the cherry blossoms, alternating them to the inside and outside. Cut the berry stem into 5" sprigs. Glue one sprig beside each rose, angled away from it. Cut the larkspur stems to ½" and glue them evenly spaced among the previous materials.

4 Use the ribbon to make a puffy bow (see page 26) with a center loop, ten 2" loops and 11" tails; glue into the open space. Cut two 5" sprigs off the remaining ivy and the rest of the leaves off the stem. Glue a sprig angled down from each side of the bow and the leaves among the bow loops. Glue the rosebuds evenly spaced around the bow. Cut the lavender into 3"–4" sprigs and divide into clusters of three. Glue the clusters evenly spaced counter-clockwise, filling any empty spaces. Attach a wire loop hanger (see page 18) to the top back.

Larkspur & Dogwood

14" round dried sage green salal/white larkspur wreath*

1 stem of peach silk dogwood with five 4" wide blossoms and many leaves

2 oz. of dried curly ting ting

½ oz. of burgundy dried baby's breath

2⅔ yards of 2" wide sage green/peach tapestry ribbon

24-gauge wire

low temperature glue gun and sticks

*or use a wreath ring to make a salal and larkspur wreath if you are unable to find one in your area.

1 Cut the dogwood blossoms into 5" sprigs. Glue one to the center top and one 1½"–2" away on each side. Glue a sprig to the left center and another 1" below it. Glue any extra leaves around the blossoms.

2 Use the ribbon to make a puffy bow (see page 26) with a center loop, ten 3" loops and 14" tails. Glue it to the upper left side between the dogwood sprigs. Clip 4–5 small salal leaves from the wreath back and glue among the bow loops. Weave a bow tail upward among the dogwood blossoms and the other downward.

3 Cut the ting ting into 9"–12" sprigs; divide into groups of 2–3 sprigs and glue evenly spaced among the bow loops and dogwood blossoms.

4 Cut the baby's breath into 3"–5" sprigs. Glue evenly spaced among the bow loops and dogwood. From the back of the wreath, cut four or five 3"–5" larkspur sprigs and glue among the bow loops. Attach a wire loop hanger (see page 18) to the upper back.

Gold 'n' Poinsettia Wreath

14" round green preserved cedar/salal/huckleberry wreath
2 white snow-glazed silk poinsettia picks, each with a 6" wide blossom, a 1½" gold pomegranate, seven ⅜" wide white berries and many 3"–4½" long leaves
fifteen 1"–1¾" wide white dried strawflower blossoms
2 yards of 1⅝" wide gold wired mesh ribbon
1 oz. of gold sparkled dried German statice
24 -gauge wire
low temperature glue gun and sticks

1 Cut 25" of ribbon and six 6" wire lengths. Twist a wire around each ribbon end and at 5" intervals between the ends. Insert one wired end through the wreath front at the left center and secure to the frame. Repeat every 4", puffing the ribbon between the wired areas as shown.

2 Lay the poinsettia picks end to end on the wreath front with a 6" gap between the blossoms. Bend them to fit the wreath curve and wire securely in place.

3 Use the remaining ribbon to make a puffy bow (see page 26) with a center loop, six 3½" loops and no tails. Glue the bow between the poinsettias. Cut the statice into 2"–4" sprigs and glue evenly spaced among the poinsettias and leaves.

4 Cut the strawflower stems to 1". Glue around the poinsettias, pomegranates and bow, using larger blossoms near the bow and smaller blossoms near the tips of the picks. Attach a wire loop hanger (see page 18) to the upper back.

Christmas Wreath

24" round wild birch wreath*, with or without leaves
4¾ yards of 2⅝" wide burgundy crushed velvet wire-edged ribbon with a gold lamé back
2 stems of latex apples, each with a 2" whole and a 2" half red/green apple, a 4" and a 2½" wide white blossom, seven ½"–¾" wide burgundy/green berries and many 2"–4" grape leaves
2 stems of artificial blackberries, each with an 11" section of ½" berries and many leaves
6–8 oz. of green preserved cedar
3 oz. of dried bell reed
six 3"–4" long dried cinnamon sticks
14-gauge wire
low temperature glue gun and sticks

*or use two vine wreaths: Take one apart, cut the branches into curving lengths and glue or wire to extend clockwise around the outer and front edges of the other wreath.

1 Attach a wire loop hanger (see page 18) to the upper back of the wreath. Cut eight 5"–14" long twigs from the back and save for step 4. Use the ribbon to make an oblong bow (see page 26) with a center loop, eight 3"–5½" loops, a 32" and a 36" tail. Glue to the wreath at the upper left. Knot each tail 3" from the end and wire them together 12" from the end of the longer tail. Attach the wire to the inner right side of the wreath.

2 Cut one 4" and two 6" cedar sprigs. Glue the 4" sprig below the bow angled right and the 6" sprigs extending left from beneath the bow loops. Glue the remaining cedar along the wreath from the bow to the lower right side.

3 Cut each apple stem to 17". Cut the whole apple and bud off one stem; glue the apple below the bow and the bud angled left from beneath the bow. Glue the rest of that stem extending right from under the bow, bending it to follow the curve of the wreath. Glue the second stem beyond the first, bending it in the same way.

4 Cut each berry stem to 12". Glue one beside the first apple stem, extending right. Cut one 5-berry sprig from the other stem and glue under the bow extending left. Glue the remainder of that stem beside the second apple stem. Cut the bell reed into 8"–10" sprigs; glue them and the twigs from step 1 evenly spaced among all the materials. Glue a 3" cinnamon stick extending left from under the bow and the rest evenly spaced among the materials on the right.

Harvest Wreath

30" wild birch wreath* with moss
2 yards of 2¾" wide gold/brown wire-edged
  ribbon
2 stems of yellow silk sunflowers, each with
  one 5" wide blossom and 3 leaves
1 stem of cream silk sunflowers with one 5"
  wide blossom and 3 leaves
2 stems of rust/green artificial berries, each
  with a 12" section of ⅜" berries and 2½"
  long leaves
2 stems of rust/brown/orange silk fall leaves,
  each with five 2"–3" long leaves, 2 berry
  sprigs and rust cornsilk
2 stems of fall-colored latex fruit, each with a
  2" wide half peach, 2 blackberries, a 1¾"
  brown plum, various berries and three
  3"–4" wide green leaves
one 5" wide orange/green latex gourd with 4
  leaves
one 3" tall yellow latex pear
1 rust latex plum pick with two 2½" long
  plums
2 oz. of dried bearded wheat
gold spray paint
30-gauge wire, 24-gauge wire
low temperature glue gun and sticks

*or use two vine wreaths: Take one apart,
cut the branches into curving lengths and glue
or wire to extend clockwise around the outer
and front edges of the other wreath.

1 Hold the sunflowers together at varying heights; wire them together 12" from the top. Don't cut the wire. Position the fall leaf stems among the sunflowers, one on each side of the center flower, again at varying heights, and wire to secure.

2 Position the berry stems as for the fall leaves; wire. Wire one fruit stem at the center front between the two side flowers. Arrange the berries and leaves to extend forward among the flowers. Cut the stems to extend 7"–9" below the wire. Wire the bouquet to the wreath as shown.

3 Use the ribbon to make a puffy bow (see page 26) with a center loop, two 4" loops, a 16" and a 27" tail. Glue it over the bouquet wire with the short tail extending left. Glue the gourd below and slightly right of the bow.

4 Glue the other fruit stem extending to the right from under the gourd. Glue the pear below the fruit pick and the plum pick below the gourd. Spray the wheat lightly with gold paint and let dry. Cut into 5"–12" sprigs and glue evenly spaced near materials of similar lengths. Attach a wire loop hanger (see page 18) to the upper back.

Garden Grapevine Wreath

24" round grapevine wreath
3½ yards of 1⅜" wide blue/burgundy/
   green flowered ribbon
3 stems of blue/purple silk delphiniums,
   each with a 22" section of ½"–2" wide
   blossoms and 4 leaves
3 stems of white silk and latex morning
   glories, each with two 3" wide blossoms,
   a bud and 11 leaves
1 stem of burgundy latex grapes with a 13"
   section of ½"–¾" wide grapes, 4 leaves
   and a wired twig
24-gauge wire
low temperature glue gun and sticks

1 Cut five 36" long vines from the wreath (smaller vines are easier to remove); set aside. Cut two delphiniums to 23". Glue one extending up the left side of the wreath nearly to the center top. Glue the other below and left of it.

2 Cut the morning glory stems to 13". Glue one to extend up the left side and over the center top of the wreath. Glue one between the delphiniums. Glue the last below the first delphinium curving downward along the lower inside of the wreath. Use the ribbon to make a puffy bow (see page 26) with a center loop, ten 3¾" loops, a 16" and a 25" tail. Glue at the lower left. Loop and glue the 16" tail upward among the flowers. Make a long loop with the 25" tail and glue it below the bow, letting the tail dangle.

3 Cut the upper 11" off the last delphinium and glue to extend downward past the center bottom. Cut the leaves off the stem; cut the rest into two 3-flower sprigs. Glue one below the bow, the other above and right of the bow. Glue a leaf near each short sprig and two near the 11" sprig.

4 Cut the top 7" off the grape stem. Glue it below the bow over the delphinium. Cut the leaf sprig off the grape stem and glue below the bow to extend among the grapes. Cut the remaining grape sprig to 8" and glue just

above and left of the bow to extend upward. Position the grapevines from step 1 over the flowers, gluing the ends among the wreath vines to secure. Attach a wire hanger (see page 18) to the upper back.

Roses & Cherries

19" round grapevine wreath
3 stems of mauve silk snapdragons, each
   with an 18" section of blossoms and
   leaves
3 stems of ivory silk roses, each with three
   2"–3" wide blossoms and many leaves
2 stems of burgundy latex cherries, each
   with 3 sprigs of two to five ¾"–1"
   cherries and 3–6 leaves
1 oz. of green preserved plumosus
½ oz. of green sheet moss
24-gauge wire
low temperature glue gun and sticks

1 Cut the binding vine or wires off the wreath and discard. Pull six vines from the wreath and set aside for step 4. Loosen the vines at the wreath bottom to make that area 6" deep. Wire the top together, pulling the vines tight and allowing the lower vines to separate.

2 Cut two snapdragon stems to 18" and one to 14". Wire an 18" stem to the lower right of the wreath, extending from between the vines and angling down to the left. Wire the other 18" stem upright on the right side of the wreath, extending over the wreath front. Wire the 14" stem near the upright stem, angled left. Cut the remaining leaf sprig from the 14" stem to 6" and glue angled left from the lower right front of the wreath.

3 Cut one cherry stem to 23" and wire extending upright between the upper snapdragon stems. Cut the lower 3-cherry sprig off the other stem and set aside. Cut the rest of the stem to 20" and wire extending along the inside wreath bottom. Glue the 3-cherry sprig outside the lower right of the wreath. Cut a rose stem to 12" and one to 16". Glue the 16" stem between the upper snapdragons and the 12" to the right of them. Cut a rose to 13" and glue angled left in front of the lower snapdragon.

4 Cut two 20" plumosus sprigs; glue one extending from behind the upper cherry and the other extending from behind the lower snapdragon. Glue 6"–14" plumosus sprigs near flowers of similar lengths. Glue the grapevines from step 1 to extend at varied heights from the lower right over the wreath front and right flowers. Glue moss tufts to cover any exposed glue or wires. Attach a wire loop hanger (see page 18) to the top back.

Heart Wreath

19" wide TWIGS™ heart wreath
with a vine lattice back

3 yards of 2½" wide burgundy/brown
printed sheer non-woven ribbon

4 stems of burgundy silk ruffled roses,
each with a 4" wide blossom and
two 5-leaf sprigs

3 stems of pink silk roses, each with a
10" section of fourteen ⅜"–⅞"
wide blossoms and many leaves

1 green silk piggyback plant with 8
branches of 1"–2" leaves

2 wired stems of brown seed pods, each
with 3 sprigs of one 3" long and
three 1½" long pods and 3 leaves

1 oz. of dried nigella

2 oz. of dark green dried bloom broom

24-gauge wire

low temperature glue gun and sticks

1 Cut the branches off the piggyback plant and to 6" long. Glue two to the heart center top, one extending upward and one downward. Glue three branches to each heart shoulder, all angled toward the sides. Cut two rose stems to 11" and two to 8". Curve one of each and wire to the left shoulder of the heart as shown, with the 8" stem closest to the center. Repeat with the other two stems on the other side.

2 Cut each pink rose stem into two 6" sprigs, one with six blossoms and one with eight. Glue one on each side of the heart below the last rose. Glue two at the heart center, one extending upward and one downward. Glue one to the top of each heart shoulder between the burgundy roses. Cut each seed pod stem into three 5" sprigs. Glue one next to each pink rose sprig.

3 Use the ribbon to make an oblong bow (see page 26) with a center loop, four 3", two 4" and two 5" loops and 20" tails. Glue to the center top; pull a tail to each side, then loop and glue it among the flowers.

4 Cut the bloom broom into 3"–4" sprigs; glue them in clusters among the flowers and leaves. Glue more clusters over the outside and inside of the wreath. Cut the nigella with 3" stems. Glue them evenly spaced among all the flowers. Attach a wire loop hanger (see page 18) to the upper back.

Pine Cone Wreath

14" round pine cone wreath*
1 stem of cream latex magnolias with
    a 4" tall closed blossom, a bud, a
    seed pod and 6 gold-brushed leaves
1 stem of dusty green silk holly with
    five 8"–10" sprigs of 3" long
    leaves, 3/8" red berries and wired
    twigs
three 6"–7" long brown feathers
2 brown dried eskira pods
two 5 1/2"x3 1/2" dried sponge
    mushrooms
1 1/4 yards of 1 3/8" wide brown/red/
    green tapestry ribbon
24-gauge wire
low temperature glue gun and sticks

*or make your own (see page 131 for
instructions and materials).

1 Wire a hanger (see page 18) to the top back of the wreath.
Glue the two sponge mushrooms among the cones at the center bottom, one over the other, as shown. Cut the stem of the magnolia blossom to 1"; glue it left of the top mushroom, extending forward. Gently loosen the petals.

2 Cut the magnolia bud to 6" and glue to extend right from under the blossom. Cut the seed pod to 9 1/2"; glue it to extend up the left side of the wreath with the stem among the cones and the pod extending forward over the blossom. Cut the magnolia leaves off the stem and glue five around the blossoms and buds as shown.

3 Cut one 12", one 7", one 3" and two 5" holly sprigs. Gently curl the twigs. Glue the 12" sprig to extend up

the left side of the wreath with the 7" sprig in front of it. Glue a 5" sprig on each side of the magnolia and the 3" sprig below it. Glue two leftover holly leaves to the lower mushroom and two left of and behind the magnolia blossom.

4 Use the ribbon to make a puffy bow (see page 26) with a center loop, four 2 3/4" loops and 7" tails. Glue to the top mushroom, just right of the magnolia blossom; bring the left tail out between the mushrooms and glue. Glue a feather in front of the 7" holly stem, one just left of the magnolia blossom and one angled forward right of the bud. Glue an eskira pod behind the magnolia blossom and one between the mushrooms under the bud.

Christmas Candle Rings

two 8" round green vinyl fir wreaths
two 11" tall black metal/glass hurricane candle holders
2⅓ yards of ⅛" wide burgundy satin twisted cord
2⅓ yards of ⅜" wide wired gold mesh braid
4 cone/rose/gift Christmas picks, each with a 2" wide bur-
    gundy/gold pine cone, a 1"x1" wrapped gift, a 1" wide
    burgundy dried rose, three 2" vinyl fir sprigs and a cluster
    of six 2½" metallic gold daisies
2 gold-brushed cone/pod/nut picks, each with a 2" long pine
    cone, 4 sprigs of assorted ½"–1" nuts and pods, three
    2½" long vinyl pine sprigs and three 3" green silk holly
    leaves
2 oz. of green preserved plumosus
24-gauge wire
low temperature glue gun and sticks

1 **For each candle ring:** Cut the components off two cone/rose/gift picks, leaving a ½" stem on each. Glue one cone to each side of a wreath. Repeat with two gifts, positioning them opposite each other between the cones. Glue a rose on each side, placed between a cone and a gift. Glue the holly leaves and fir sprigs evenly spaced around the ring. Set aside the daisies for step 3.

2 Cut apart a cone/pod/nut pick. Glue the components evenly spaced around the ring, tucking them among the fir sprigs and the components from step 1.

3 Cut the daisy clusters into individual stems. Glue them evenly spaced around the ring among the fir sprigs and pick components. Cut the plumosus into 2½"–3½" sprigs. Glue them among the fir sprigs and components, angling them outward around the outside of the ring and upward among the other materials. Cut seven 6" lengths each of braid and cord. Hold one length of each together and form into a loop; wire the ends. Repeat to make a total of seven double loops, then glue them evenly spaced throughout the ring. Remove the chimney from the hurricane, place the ring around the base, insert the candle and replace the chimney.

Vine Wreaths

Grapevine wreaths are everywhere! Craft stores are overflowing with them, whether plain or lacquered or painted, and in sizes from a very small 4" to a huge 36" wide. And they are so versatile! Vine wreaths are pretty when completely covered with dried and silk floral materials, or when decorated with a crescent design, which leaves the wreath partially uncovered.

The dark vines of lacquered wreaths add shine to a design, providing a wonderful base for romantic, woodsy, or even Christmas designs. Natural grapevine wreaths add a rustic feeling to designs with the rough bark and twirling tendrils. Some vines even have peeling bark, adding more texture and interest to a design. And many times dried leaves will still be clinging to the vines, making a terrific base for a traditional, rustic or country design.

Most of the designs in this section are made on grapevine wreaths because of their accessibility, but nearly all can be created on any type of vine wreath. We've found winged elm and honeysuckle vines made into wreaths, as well as buckbrush and bittersweet. If your regional craft store carries a wreath constructed from a vine found in your area, try creating your design on it. The results will be beautiful—and hold special meaning for you as well!

Although each design in this section involves at least one vine wreath, they are all very unique and feature some unusual techniques. The Birdhouse Wreath on page 48 is designed with the wreath lying flat on the table, forming a wonderful base for the centerpiece. The Grass & Nest Centerpiece on page 50 is another centerpiece, this one overflowing with grassy textures. It brings to mind a walk through a meadow, especially with the discovery of the bird's nest tucked among the grass. The centerpiece looks great in the middle of a kitchen table or against a wall on a hall table.

Putting two or more wreaths together for a design is a technique we've used several times to produce an unusual base. The Standing Wreath on page 52 utilizes a small rattan wreath as a horizontal base, allowing a larger one to stand upright in its center. On page 57 in the Swag Of Wreaths, five small vine wreaths are attached to make a garland or swag, creating the perfect addition to a horizontal wall space that needs a sweet, delicate decoration.

Two vine hearts were wired together to form the base for the Double Heart on page 49, creating another unique base for designing. Adding the dried and silk floral materials along with a lacy ribbon resulted in a pretty, romantic wall piece.

For other unique looks, try putting wreaths together with different bases. A wreath can be attached to a swag, an arch, or a larger wreath for some unusual beginnings to beautiful designs. For another approach, try attaching other items such as bird cages, garlands or baskets to wreaths, then decorating both elements to coordinate with and complement each other.

A great technique in floral designing is to use an unusual component when creating a piece. While pine is nearly always used for Christmas designs, the project on page 51, Autumn In The Garden, presents a delightful wreath to display year-round. The pine provides a deep hunter green to complement the rust and lighter green tones of the fruit and berries, while also reinforcing the established lines of the design.

Birds, nests, raffia, moss, mushrooms and pretty ribbons, along with dried and silk flowers, all enhance the twelve designs in this Vine Wreath section. The arrangements of and techniques for attaching those components work together to create the wonderful array of lovely designs found on these pages.

Eucalyptus Wreath with Birds

8" wide grapevine wreath
two 2⅛" long blue/mauve
  mushroom sparrows
2" wide dried grass bird's nest
three ½" long brown speckled
  plastic eggs
nine 9" stems of green
  preserved eucalyptus
1 stem of blue silk yarrow
  with three 7" sprigs of
  many 1"–1½" wide pellet-
  like blossom clusters
2 oz. of dried brisa maxima
eight 48" strands of mauve
  raffia
eight 48" strands of natural
  raffia
24 gauge wire
low temperature glue gun and
  sticks

1 Hold together four strands of each raffia color and glue to the bottom front of the wreath 8–10" from one end. Wrap the long ends around the wreath spiral fashion with the wraps 1½" apart; glue to secure and trim the ends to 8–10". Cut the eucalyptus to these lengths: two 9", two 7", two 6", six 4½". Glue a 9" sprig extending outward on each side with a 6" and a 7" above it. Glue one 4½" sprig above and two below the longer sprigs on each side.

2 Save six stems of brisa maxima for step 4. Cut the rest to 6"–8" and glue among the eucalyptus, following the same lines. Bend a 2" wire length into a U and insert through the bottom of the nest. Wire the nest to the inside bottom of the wreath. Glue the eggs into the nest.

3 Cut two 7" yarrow sprigs. Glue one above the 9" eucalyptus on each side. Cut the rest into 4"–6" sprigs and glue among the eucalyptus near materials of similar lengths. Cut the remaining raffia to 24" and hold together. Use a single piece to tie the strands together 5"–6" from one end. Divide into three even bunches and and braid to within 5"–6" from the other end; secure. Use the braid to make a collar bow (see page 24) with 3" loops; glue below the nest.

4 Glue one bird to the inside of the wreath just right of the nest. Glue the other to the left front above the arrangement. Cut the baby's breath into 1"–2" sprigs and glue them evenly spaced throughout the floral materials. Cut the remaining brisa maxima to 1" and glue around the bow. Attach a wire hanger (see page 18) to the top back.

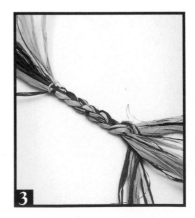

Southwest Wreath

18" round grapevine wreath
2 stems of dusty green silk
    eucalyptus, each with three
    7"–9" branches of many
    4"–5" sprigs of leaves
3 yards of 2½" ivory/green/
    mauve tapestry wire-edged
    ribbon
1 stem of mauve silk
    magnolias with five 5"
    wide blossoms and leaves
6 dried star cones on picks
1 stem of dried bell reed with
    many blossom clusters
1 oz. of dried rice grass
24-gauge wire
white spray paint
low temperature glue gun and
    sticks

1 For a white-washed effect, lightly spray the wreath with paint. Cut the eucalyptus stems to 12", then wire them to the middle and lower right front of the wreath, leaving a 6" empty space between.

2 Make a puffy bow (see page 26) with a center loop, six 4½" loops and two 14" tails. Cut the magnolias off the main branch, leaving a 4" stem on each. Glue two above the bow, one nestled in the center bow loop and two below the bow.

3 Cut the star cone stems to 3". Glue one near each magnolia and one among the lower bow loops. Cut the bell reed into 3"–5" sprigs. Glue clusters of 1–3 sprigs evenly spaced among the magnolias and star cones as shown.

4 Cut the rice grass into 3"–4" sprigs. Glue clusters of 4–5 sprigs throughout the arrangement, filling any empty spaces. Fold the bow tails, pulling them close to the bow as shown in the large photo. Attach a wire hanger (see page 18) to the upper back.

Birdhouse Wreath Centerpiece

4"x4½"x5" wooden birdhouse on an 8" pedestal

12" round honeysuckle wreath

3" long teal/green feathered bird

1 stem of pink silk cherry blossoms with eleven 10"–16" sprigs of ¾"–1½" flower/bud clusters

3 stems of ivory silk mini roses, each with five 1" wide flowers

1 stem of light blue silk baby's breath with three 12" sprigs of 1" wide blossoms

½ oz. of green preserved tree fern

½ oz. of white starflowers

1 oz. of American Moss® green excelsior

green floral tape

24-gauge wire

low temperature glue gun and sticks

1 Lay the wreath flat. Place the birdhouse inside the wreath and wire securely to the left side. Glue the bird to the front of the birdhouse. Glue excelsior to cover the pedestal and wire, around the bottom of the birdhouse and around the bird's feet.

2 From the cherry blossom stem, cut one 16" and two 10" sprigs. Glue the 16" sprig into the wreath, curving it over the top of the birdhouse as shown. Glue one 10" sprig directly behind the 16" sprig, extending along the back of the wreath. Wire the other 10" sprig to the wreath top, extending from the birdhouse toward the wreath front. Cut the remaining sprigs off the main stem and glue them among the other blossoms.

3 Cut a rose stem into an 11" sprig of two roses, a 5½" sprig with one rose and a 4" sprig of two roses. Insert the 11" sprig, the 5½" sprig and the 4" sprig in that order in front of the 16" cherry blossom sprig, curving them forward. Repeat with another rose stem, gluing the sprigs behind the same cherry sprig and curving these backward. Cut the remaining rose stem into 3"–5" sprigs and glue among the cherry blossoms curving forward along the wreath front. Cut a 10" sprig of baby's breath. Glue it in front of the 16" cherry sprig. Cut the remaining baby's breath into six 4"–7" sprigs and glue evenly spaced throughout the arrangement.

4 Hold the starflowers in clusters of 6–12 and trim to 3"–10" long; tape the lower 1" of stems. Cut the fern into 5"–14" sprigs. Glue the fern and starflower clusters evenly spaced throughout the arrangement near items of similar lengths.

Double Heart

two 10"x12" vine heart wreaths
2½ yards of ⅝" wide gold satin wire-edged ribbon
4 yards of ⅜" wide natural cotton wire-edged
    ribbon braid
2 stems of white silk climbing roses, each with
    four 1½"–2" wide blossoms and many leaves
1 oz. of green preserved plumosus
1 oz. of dried nigella
½ oz. of dried linum or flax
24-gauge wire
low temperature glue gun and sticks

1 Wire the wreaths together as shown. Cut six 7"–8" plumosus sprigs. Beginning at the upper left of the upper wreath, glue two sprigs curving over the top and four down the left side. Cut seven 4" sprigs and glue three to fill empty areas. Glue two extending upward along the right side of the lower heart and two extending downward.

2 Cut a 2½-yard length of braid and hold together with the gold ribbon. Handle as one to make a puffy bow (see page 26) with a center loop, eight 2¼" loops, a 16" tail and a 24" tail of each color. Wire over the stems at the upper left. Bring the 16" tails behind the upper wreath, around to the front, and glue near the bottom point. Weave the 24" tails through the wreaths as shown and glue over the plumosus stems on the lower wreath. Use the remaining

braid to make a puffy bow with a center loop, six 2" loops and two 7" tails. Wire to the lower wreath over the 24" tails.

3 Cut each rose with a 1" stem. Glue a large rose just above the upper bow, one to the right of and one below the bow. Repeat on the lower wreath. Glue one small rose at the top of the upper wreath and one halfway down the left side.

4 Cut the nigella into 1" sprigs. Glue evenly spaced throughout the design with the larger heads near the bows and smaller heads near the plumosus tips. Cut the linum into 1"–3" sprigs and glue evenly spaced throughout the design, filling any empty spaces. Attach a wire hanger (see page 18) behind the right shoulder of the upper heart.

Grass & Nest Centerpiece

12" round grapevine wreath
3 ⅓ yards of ³⁄₁₆" wide green
   jute cord
twelve 48" long strands of raffia
1 ½ oz. of dried amaranthus
1 oz. of green preserved
   myrtle
4 oz. of white dried ti tree
   branches
1 oz. of green dried lino grass
1 oz. of dried rice grass
2"x3"x1" block of floral foam
   for silks
½ oz. of green sheet moss
3" wide grass bird's nest
two 1" long speckled eggs
24-gauge wire
low temperature glue gun and
   sticks

1 Cut the foam into a 2"x2"x1" block and a 2"x1"x1" block. Wrap each block with moss and wire to the wreath opposite each other with the larger block on the left; save the remaining moss for step 4. Save three 1"–3" sprigs of each dried material for step 4. Divide the remainder into thirds—⅔ will be used for the left area and ⅓ for the right area. Cut the amaranthus for the left area into 4"–11" sprigs. Insert longer sprigs into the foam center and shorter ones around the edges, angled over the wreath, with medium sprigs filling in between. Repeat on the right, but cut the sprigs to 3"–7".

2 Cut the myrtle and ti tree branches as for the amaranthus. Insert evenly spaced near sprigs of similar lengths.

3 Cut the lino grass into 3"–11" sprigs. Glue the sprigs spaced evenly throughout both design areas near materials of similar lengths. Cut the rice grass into 6"–16" sprigs for the left area and 5"–9" for the right area. Insert them evenly spaced throughout.

4 Use your fingernail to shred the raffia into thin strands. Divide the strands into three bunches. Tie the bunches together end to end to make a very long strand. Wrap the cord with the raffia, tying the ends to secure. Use one end of the cord to make a loopy bow (see page 27) with six 3" loops and a 6" tail; at the other end make a loopy bow with six 2" loops and a 6" tail. Glue the large bow to the front of the left area, angled outward. Wrap the cord spiral fashion around the wreath front and glue the small bow to the wreath behind the right area. Glue the nest just right of the large bow. Glue the eggs into the nest. Glue the reserved sprigs around the nest as shown in the large photo. Glue tufts of moss around the eggs and spaced along the wreath top.

14"x17" TWIGS™ oval wreath with a vine lattice back
2 stems of green vinyl pine, each with three 10" branches of eight 5"–7" sprigs
3 grape picks with many ½"–¾" wide transparent amber acrylic grapes and leaves
3 stems of mixed artificial fruit, each with one 2" wide pomegranate, one 1¼" wide pear, five
  ⅝"–¾" nuts and berries, and many leaves
1½ yards of 1⅜" wide rust/green/cream floral print ribbon
1 oz. of dried brisa maxima
24-gauge wire, low temperature glue gun and sticks

1 Cut the branches off the pine stems. Cut two branches to 9" long and wire to the center top of the wreath with one extending down each side to the wreath center. Cut two branches to 7" long and wire to the wreath bottom with one extending up each side to within 2" of the upper branch. Cut each of the two remaining branches into eight 5"–7" sprigs. Set eight aside for step 3. Glue the rest evenly spaced throughout the lower branches to create a fuller appearance.

2 Cut two fruit stems to 12" and wire them end to end over the upper pine with a 2" gap between the lowest fruits. Cut the remaining fruit stem into two 7" sprigs. Wire them end to end to the wreath bottom. Wire a grape pick over the center of each upper fruit stem; wire the third to the left bottom.

3 Use the ribbon to make an oblong bow (see page 26) with a center loop, four 2½"–3" loops and 14" tails; glue to the wreath top and weave a tail down each side among the fruits. Cut three reserved pine sprigs in half so you have eleven 2½"–7" sprigs. Glue longer sprigs around the bow and short sprigs among the loops. Cut the berries into 3"–4" sprigs. Glue them evenly spaced throughout the upper and lower design areas.

4 Cut the brisa into 3"–7" sprigs; glue evenly spaced and near previous materials of similar lengths. Attach a wire hanger (see page 18) to the back of the wreath.

Standing Wreath

2 round rattan wreaths: one 6", one 10" wide
2½" wide grass bird's nest
two 1" long plastic speckled eggs
1 stem of purple silk wisteria with
    four 5" long blossom clusters
    and thirteen 7" leaf sprigs
ten 1" wide pink dried roses
1 oz. of dried nigella
½ oz. of green preserved sprengeri
1 oz. of dried Siberian statice
24-gauge wire
low temperature glue gun and
    sticks

1 Place the 6" wreath flat on the table, then wire and glue the 10" wreath into the center as shown. Cut all thirteen wisteria leaf sprigs off the stem and glue as shown, working from the top down so each sprig covers the stem of the previous sprig. Keep the left arrangement slightly shorter than the right one, as shown.

2 Cut the blossom clusters off the wisteria stem. Glue three extending in a fan upward from the center bottom; glue the last to the center right front. Cut the sprengeri into 3"–7" sprigs; set two aside for step 4. Glue the remaining sprengeri evenly spaced among the wisteria blossoms and leaves.

3 Glue the nest to the center of the base as shown. Cut the rose stems to 5". Glue 2"–3" apart among the wisteria blossoms and leaves, using smaller roses near the tips and larger ones around the nest. Repeat with the nigella, spacing the pods evenly throughout the design.

4 Cut the statice into 1"–4" sprigs. Glue three or four 1" sprigs into the nest. Glue the rest evenly spaced among all the previous materials, using shorter sprigs around the nest and longer ones extending up the wreath sides. Cut the reserved sprengeri sprigs to 2"; glue them and the eggs into the nest.

Peony Garden Wreath

22" round grapevine wreath
1 oz. of dried dwarf's beard
 lichen
1 green/burgundy artificial wild
 grape branch with 5 clusters
 of ½"–¾" wide grapes and
 many leaves and branches
three 5"–6" wide dried sponge
 mushrooms on picks
5 burgundy dried peonies
3 oz. of pink dried ti tree
 branches
1 oz. of green preserved
 princess pine
1 oz. of dried German statice
24-gauge wire
low temperature glue gun and
 sticks

1 Divide the lichen into thirds; glue one third on the left wreath front. Cut the two lowest grape/foliage clusters off the grape branch. Lay the branch over the lichen, bending it to match the wreath's curve. Wire in place, then pull the lichen up through the grape foliage.

2 Cut the mushroom picks to 2"; glue one where the grapes were removed, one at the center bottom and one between the others. Tuck half of the remaining lichen around the mushrooms. Glue the smaller grape cluster from step 1 spilling off the right of the lowest mushroom and the larger cluster left of the center mushroom.

3 Soak the peony heads in warm water for 15 minutes to soften them; blot excess water. Cut six lower petals from the blossom backs, then shape the blossoms and glue them to the left side, angled as shown. Cut six 1½"–2½" ti tree sprigs; glue them extending up from the center of the bottom mushroom. Cut the remaining ti tree into 4"–8" sprigs; glue them evenly spaced among the peonies and grapes. Cut the pine into 1"–2" sprigs; glue them evenly spaced among the peonies, behind the mushrooms and near the grape clusters. Glue the reserved peony petals to the middle mushroom.

4 Cut the statice into 1"–5" sprigs; glue evenly spaced among all the materials. Tuck the remaining lichen through the materials. Attach a wire loop hanger (see page 18) to the top back.

Peach Dogwood Wreath

14" round lacquered vine wreath

2 stems of green/burgundy silk grape leaves, each with a 15" section of 2"–3½" wide leaves

2 stems of burgundy acrylic raspberries, each with 4 sprigs of three ½"–¾" wide berries and many leaves

2 stems of peach silk dogwood, each with five 4" wide blossoms and many leaves

2 stems of silk Queen Anne's lace, each with twelve 1"–2" wide clusters of ⅜" wide blossoms

24-gauge wire

low temperature glue gun and sticks

1 Weave the base of a grape leaf stem into the wreath vines at the center top; bend the branch to follow the curve of the wreath and wire in place. Repeat with the other stem on the opposite side; shape the foliage as shown.

2 Cut each raspberry stem into four 4"–6" sprigs. Glue them evenly spaced among the grape leaves.

3 Cut the dogwood into 3"–4" sprigs. Glue 1"–2" apart among the leaves as shown.

4 Cut the Queen Anne's lace into 1"–3" sprigs. Glue the sprigs evenly spaced among all the previous materials. Attach a wire loop hanger (see page 18) to the top back.

Spring Garden

18" round grapevine wreath

1 green silk ivy bush with six 9", six 6" and six 4" branches of many 1"–2" wide leaves

1 stem of yellow and 1 stem of burgundy silk epidendrum, each 12" long with three 3" blossoms, a 1" bud, many leaves and roots

one 14" long stem of white silk wild narcissus with 2 stems of five 1¾" blossoms, many leaves and a 1½" bulb with roots

1 stem of white and 1 stem of blue silk wild hyacinth, each 12" long with many 1" wide blossoms, 3 leaves and a 2" bulb with roots

1 stem of yellow artificial wild daisy with a 15" and two 13" long sprigs of many ¾" wide blossoms

1 oz. of dried forest flower (gray/black) lichen

24-gauge wire

low temperature glue gun and sticks

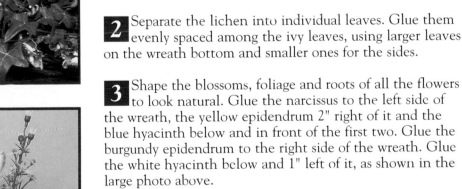

1 Cut all the branches off the ivy bush. Set the 4" branches aside for step 4. Wire a 9" branch to the right center of the wreath extending up; wire another 3" below the first and another 3" below the second. Continue down the wreath with three 6" sprigs, ending with the stem of the last sprig at the center bottom. Repeat on the other side. Attach a wire loop hanger (see page 18) to the top back.

2 Separate the lichen into individual leaves. Glue them evenly spaced among the ivy leaves, using larger leaves on the wreath bottom and smaller ones for the sides.

3 Shape the blossoms, foliage and roots of all the flowers to look natural. Glue the narcissus to the left side of the wreath, the yellow epidendrum 2" right of it and the blue hyacinth below and in front of the first two. Glue the burgundy epidendrum to the right side of the wreath. Glue the white hyacinth below and 1" left of it, as shown in the large photo above.

4 Cut the daisy stem into one 13", two 9", one 6" and two 4" sprigs. Glue a 9" sprig on each side of the burgundy epidendrum. Glue a 4" sprig right of the white hyacinth. Glue the 13" and 6" sprigs left of the narcissus; glue a 4" sprig right of the blue hyacinth. Glue the 4" ivy sprigs evenly spaced among the bulbs.

Trailing Heart

12" lacquered vine heart with tail and pocket
1 green silk ivy bush with seven 6" branches of many
   ½"–¾" wide leaves
two 10" long lavender parchment miniature rose/berry
   swags, each with five ¾"–1" wide roses, ten ⅜"wide
   berries, four 2" long foliage spikes with pink blossoms
   and eight 1"–1½" long leaves
1 stem of dark pink silk miniature anemones with four
   1½" wide blossoms
1 yard of ³⁄₁₆" wide mauve picot satin ribbon
1 yard of ³⁄₁₆" wide lavender picot satin ribbon
1 yard of ⅜" wide white satin ribbon
¼ oz. of green sheet moss
1 oz. of mauve starflowers
one 2⅛" long mauve mushroom sparrow
two ⅞" long mauve mushroom baby sparrows
2" wide grass bird's nest
2"x2"x1" block of floral foam for drieds, 24-gauge wire
low temperature glue gun and sticks

1 Cover the sides of the foam with moss; insert into the pocket of the heart. Glue a small moss tuft into the nest bottom. Glue the nest to the pocket rim just right of the center, angled forward. Attach a wire loop hanger (see page 18) to the wreath back.

2 Cut the ivy into 6" branches. Set one aside for step 4. Insert one extending forward behind the nest on the right side, two extending up from the foam center and three cascading over the pocket rim. Cut each swag in half, creating four 5" sprigs. Wire two sprigs together stem to tip and insert into the foam center extending upward. Insert a sprig between the long sprig and the nest and another angling down over the lower ivy as shown.

3 Glue the large sparrow to the right shoulder of the heart and the baby sparrows into the nest. Hold all three ribbons together and handle as one to make a puffy bow (see page 26) with a center loop, six 2" loops, a 7" tail and a 5" tail of each color. Glue the bow left of the nest. Cut one anemone stem to 5" and insert between the upper swag sprigs. Cut three anemone stems to 2"; insert one below the 5" sprig, one among the left bow loops and one among the right bow loops.

4 Hold 3–6 starflowers together and cut the stems to 1"–5". Glue in a cluster among materials of similar lengths. Repeat to fill evenly among the materials. Cut the ivy leaves off the remaining sprig and glue evenly spaced in the center of the design.

Swag of Wreaths

five 4" round grapevine wreaths
1 green silk mini ivy bush with seven 5" long branches of many ½"–¾" wide leaves
1 stem of white silk wild daisies with two 13" long sprigs and a 15" long sprig, each with many ¾"
   wide blossoms
1 oz. of pink dried starflowers
½ oz. of dried rice grass
six 48" long strands of raffia
24-gauge wire
low temperature glue gun and sticks

1 Lay the wreaths on a flat surface in a slight arc with the sides touching; wire together where they touch. Cut the ivy into 5" branches. Beginning at the center top of the middle wreath, glue end to end in a serpentine toward the last wreath as shown. Repeat on the other end.

2 Use four strands of raffia to make a loopy bow (see page 27) with 2" loops and 20" tails; use your fingernail to shred the loops and tails. Glue the bow to the top of the center wreath and weave the tails through the ivy on both ends to extend 3"–4" beyond the end as shown. Trim excess and set aside for step 4. Cut the remaining 48" strands in half, fold each half in half again and tie one to each end of the swag for a hanger; shred.

3 Cut the daisy stem into 1"–2" sprigs, each with 2–3 blossoms. Glue the sprigs among the ivy leaves, extending in the same directions.

4 Cut the starflowers to 1½"–2" long; glue in clusters of 3–4 evenly spaced around the bow and throughout the previous materials. Repeat with 2"–3" sprigs of rice grass as shown in the large photo. Cut the remaining raffia into 6"–12" lengths and glue below the bow center for additional tails. Cut off a hidden ivy leaf and glue to the bow center.

Wreaths Taken A·P·A·R·T

Each project in this section began with an average, commonplace wreath available from a craft store. By cutting, reshaping, wiring and gluing, we've formed them into new shapes or added dimension to the original shape, resulting in unusual and spectacular looks.

The swag at the left began its life as a 24" round grapevine wreath. By changing its shape, it became a gorgeous design and, because of its new size, can be used in a larger setting. Another S-shaped design, the Ivy Centerpiece & Candles on page 64 actually began as a foam heart wreath. By cutting it in half, flipping one piece over and gluing the straight ends together, it became a long centerpiece perfect for a romantic evening dinner.

For four designs within this section, vines have been cut from the bases or from additional wreaths, then wired and glued as new elements in the designs. The results are distinctive creating unique pieces which look terrific in different decor styles.

Wreaths make great bases when used as purchased. However, exceptional looks can be achieved by taking them apart and using the pieces in unusual ways before adding other design elements. Don't be afraid of pulling the vines apart, cutting elements out of the base or adding new materials to a plain base—spectacular designs can result!

HYDRANGEA & DOGWOOD SWAG

one 24" round grapevine wreath

3½ yards of 1½"wide blue/ mauve taffeta wire-edged ribbon

2 stems of blue silk hydrangeas, each with a 5" wide blossom head and 2 leaves

2 stems of pink silk dogwood, each with a 17" section of five 4" blossoms, 3 buds and leaves

2 branches of white silk cherry blossoms, each with a 26" section of many ½"–1½" wide blossoms

1 green silk English ivy bush with twelve 8"–18" long branches of many 1"–2" wide leaves

1 oz. of pink dried German statice

2 oz. of dried birch or buck twigs

24-gauge wire, low temperature glue gun and sticks

1 Cut the wreath in half, remove the binding and loosen the branches. Gently straighten each half to form a soft curve; wire the ends together. Repeat with 12 more vines, then position the two bundles wired ends together, overlapping the stems 10" to make a 75" long S-shaped swag. Wire again 6" on each side of the first wire to secure.

2 Use the ribbon to make an oblong bow (see page 26) with a center loop, four 4" loops, two 5" loops, two 6" loops and 22" tails. Wire to the swag center, angling the bow slightly. Pinch a ribbon tail 14" from the bow, wrap with wire and attach to the swag, looping it to drape gracefully. Repeat with the other tail on the other end as shown.

3 Cut the hydrangea stems to 5" and attach one on each side at the top left and bottom right of the bow. Cut the ivy into twelve 8"–18" branches and attach six on each side extending toward the wreath end, with the longest near the center of the swag. Cut the cherry blossom stems to 20" and wire one to each side, fanning the sprigs out among the ivy branches. Repeat with a dogwood branch on each side.

4 Cut the statice into 5"–6" sprigs and the twigs to 8"–10". Glue them evenly spaced among the floral materials, following similar angles. Attach a wire loop hanger (see page 18) to a branch at the upper back of the swag.

BOUQUET WREATH

one 22" round grapevine wreath

2½ yards of 3" wide jute open-weave wired ribbon

1 stem of purple silk Canterbury bells with seven 1" wide blossoms and 7 buds

1 stem of purple silk Japanese iris with three 4" sprigs, each with a 2½"blossom

one 3" wide dried lotus pod on a 4" pick

2 oz. of dried bromus grass

2 oz. of green preserved cedar

3 oz. of burgundy preserved spiral eucalyptus

2 oz. of dried nigella pods

2 oz. of dried lemonleaf (salal)

2 oz. of dried lepidium

1 oz. of yellow preserved sinuata statice

2 oz. of pink dried ti tree branches

24-gauge wire

low temperature glue gun and sticks

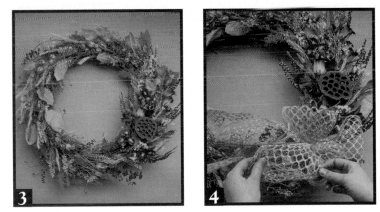

1 Cut the binding from the wreath and loosen the branches. From the back, cut six 24" pieces and set aside for step 4. Attach a wire loop hanger (see page 18) to the upper back. Cut the eucalyptus into twenty-one 6" sprigs and glue in clusters of three evenly spaced angled counter-clockwise around the wreath. Cut the cedar and bromus each into twenty 6" sprigs and glue evenly spaced around the wreath as shown.

2 Glue the lotus pod to the wreath at the 4:00 position. Cut the upper 9" off the Canterbury bells, then cut the remainder to 4". Glue the 9" sprig above the lotus pod extending upward and the 4" sprig extending left from the lotus pod. Cut the iris into three 4" sprigs and glue evenly spaced around the lotus pod.

3 Cut the ti tree into six 8" sprigs and the statice into six 4" sprigs. Glue evenly spaced among the bells and iris as shown. Cut the nigella into 25 sprigs with 5" stems and glue in clusters of five evenly spaced around the wreath. Cut the salal and lepidium into 5" sprigs and glue evenly spaced throughout the wreath, leaving an empty area at the lower right for the bow.

4 Use the ribbon to make a standup bow (see page 25) with three 4" loops and 25" tails. Glue the bow 5" below the lotus pod and stretch the ribbon of each loop to create width. Arrange the tails to extend upward as shown in the large photo. Glue the grapevines from step 1 loosely criss-crossing over the materials around the wreath.

GARDEN CENTERPIECE

one 12" round Styrofoam® wreath
6½ yards of 1" wide green burlap ribbon
1 green silk English ivy bush with seventeen 6"–10" branches of many 1"–2" wide leaves
1 stem of dark pink silk gladiolus with six 2" wide blossoms and 4 buds
1 stem of purple silk iris with three 4"–6" stems, each with a 2½" blossom and foliage
1 stem of white silk ranunculus with two 2½" blossoms and 1 bud
5 oz. of green preserved sprengeri
2 oz. of green preserved isolepsis grass
3 oz. of white dried starflowers
2 oz. of dark blue dried larkspur
2 oz. of burgundy dried linum or flax
1 oz. of green sphagnum moss
two 1" long mauve mushroom sparrows
one 2" wide grass bird's nest
one 2"x3" wooden birdhouse
low temperature glue gun and sticks

1 Cut the wreath in half, forming two arches. Wrap each arch spiral fashion with ribbon to completely cover it. Glue the ribbon ends to secure. Glue moss to cover the cut ends of each arch. Cut the gladiolus to 14"; insert and glue into the center of one arch (you may need to poke a hole in the ribbon first).

2 Cut the ivy and sprengeri into 5" sprigs and glue evenly spaced to cover both arches, leaving a space on the second arch as shown for the birdhouse. Cut the iris to 8" and glue to the right of the gladiolus.

3 Cut the ranunculus into three 5" sprigs. Glue in a triangle to the left of the gladiolus. Glue the birdhouse to the center of the other arch. Cut about 20 starflower stems to 6" long and wire the stems at the bottom. Repeat for two more 6" and ten 3" clusters.

4 Glue six 3" clusters evenly spaced among the greenery on the birdhouse arch. Glue the remaining clusters to the other arch, spacing the 6" clusters evenly among the taller flowers and the 3" clusters among the shorter foliage toward the arch ends.

5 Cut and wire the isolepsis as for the starflowers, using 15–20 grass blades per cluster. Make one 12", two 8" and four 5" long clusters. Insert and glue the 12" cluster to the left of the gladiolus, an 8" cluster on each side of the iris and the rest evenly spaced throughout the birdhouse arch.

6 Cut the larkspur into three 6" and twelve 4" sprigs. Glue the 6" and four 4" sprigs evenly spaced among the florals on the gladiolus arch, with the taller sprigs toward the center and the shorter sprigs angled toward each end. Glue any remaining sprigs evenly spaced among the florals on the birdhouse arch.

7 Cut the linum into one 12", one 8" and fifteen 4" sprigs. Glue the 12" sprig to the left to the gladiolus stem, slightly to the back, and the 8" sprig to the right of the gladiolus, also slightly to the back. Glue the remaining sprigs evenly spaced throughout both arches.

8 Glue the nest to the far right side of the gladiolus arch. Glue one bird into the nest and the other to the center of the birdhouse roof. Glue any remaining dried materials to fill any empty spaces on each arch.

ALTERNATE ARRANGEMENTS OF THE GARDEN CENTERPIECE

Ivy Centerpiece & Candles

one 12" wide Styrofoam® heart wreath
1 green silk English ivy bush with seventeen 6"–10" branches of many
 1"–2" leaves
1 green silk ivy bush with nine 12"–18" branches of many 1"–2½" leaves
6 stems of cream silk roses, each with one 2½" blossom
4 oz. of green dried sphagnum moss
6 oz. of green preserved ming fern
2 oz. of burgundy preserved heather
2 oz. of preserved stirlingia
two 3"x8" white pillar candles
20 U-shaped floral pins
four 4" wood picks
tacky craft glue, low temperature glue gun and sticks

1 Cut the heart vertically into two halves. Apply glue to one end of each wood pick and insert halfway into the straight end of a heart half. Apply more glue to the exposed pick ends and the heart end. Push the other heart half onto the picks securely to make a long S-shaped base; let dry. Cover the top and sides with the moss, securing with U-pins.

2 Cut all the ivy into 5" sprigs. Glue to evenly cover the base, alternating the two types and anchoring the stems securely into the moss and foam.

3 Cut the ming fern into forty 5" sprigs; glue evenly spaced among the ivy sprigs. Cut the rose stems to 4"; insert and glue evenly spaced, angled among the greenery as shown.

4 Cut the heather into thirteen 6" sprigs; glue evenly spaced among the florals, angling them alternately toward each side of the base. Cut the stirlingia into eighteen 4" sprigs and glue evenly spaced among the florals as shown. Place the candles inside the curves of the S as shown in the large photo above.

TERRA COTTA TRIPLET

one 12" round grapevine wreath
4 oz. of green dried sphagnum moss
4 oz. of dried lavender
7 pink dried roses with 4" stems
2 oz. of dried barley or beardless wheat
2 oz. of mauve dried starflowers
1 oz. of white dried larkspur
one 5"–6" wide head of lavender dried hydrangea
six 2½" wide terra cotta pots
two 2⅛" long blue/mauve mushroom sparrows
24-gauge wire
low temperature glue gun and sticks

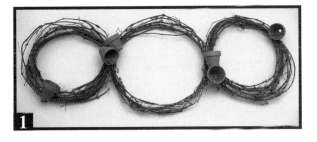

1 Remove the binding from the wreath and loosen the branches. Cut the wreath into three sections, making three wreaths, and wire them together side by side. Thread a wire through the hole in the bottom of each pot and wire each to the triplet wreath, angling them as shown. Reinforce by gluing the pots to the wreath and to each other where they touch.

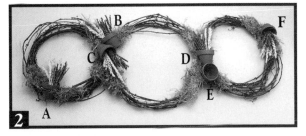

2 Glue moss into and around the pots to hide the glue and wires; glue more moss 4" on each side of each pot. Refer to the diagram to identify the pot positions. Cut the barley stems to 3" and wire together in five clusters of 5–6. Glue one into the back of each pot A, B, C, D and F. Divide the lavender into five clusters and wire the bottom of each. Glue one in front of each barley cluster.

3 Remove the blossoms from one larkspur stem and glue the blossoms into pot E. Cut the remaining larkspur stems to 3", divide into three clusters and glue one into each pot C, D and F as shown. Divide the starflowers into three clusters and glue one into the each pot B, D and F.

4 Cut the rose stems to 2". Glue four into pot A, three into the pot C and one into pot D. Glue one bird just right of pot A and the other into pot C. Divide the hydrangea head into five blossom clusters and glue one on each side of pot A, one between pots B and C, and two right of pot E. Attach wire loop hangers (see page 18) to the triplet wreath back behind pots B and D.

DRIED GARDEN ARCH

8" round wreath ring with 6
    prongs
2 oz. of dried caspia
1 oz. of green preserved
    plumosus
4 oz. of purple preserved
    statice
4 oz. of yellow preserved
    statice
4 oz. of green preserved
    eucalyptus
2 oz. of burgundy preserved
    mini baby's breath
2 oz. of burgundy preserved
    poa grass
2 oz. of dried bromus grass
10 stems of pink dried roses
4½ yards of 1⅜"wide
    burgundy/blue/green ribbon
24-gauge wire
low temperature glue gun and sticks

1   Use wire cutters to cut the wreath form near a set of prongs; trim off the excess frame near the end set of prongs. Spread the ring into an arch shape. Divide each type of dried flowers into seven equal bunches. Cut the stems to the following lengths: eucalyptus, plumosus and bromus grass to 8"–10"; caspia, purple statice and poa grass to 7"–9"; baby's breath and yellow statice to 6"–8". Place any shorter stems into the seventh bunch and set aside for step 3. **For each bouquet:** Hold one bunch each of eucalyptus, bromus, and plumosus stems together, fanning to 6" wide. Place one of each 7"–9" bunch on the fan, keeping the stem ends even; repeat with the 6"–8" drieds. Place a bouquet between the prongs on one end of the arch, with the heads extending downward and the stem ends 1"–1½" past the prongs. Fold the prongs securely over the flowers.

2 Repeat twice, placing each bouquet so the heads cover the stems of the previous bouquet. Repeat on the opposite side of the arch.

3 Use the ribbon to make a puffy bow (see page 26) with a center loop, ten 4½" loops and 14" tails. Wire the bow to the center of the arch. Glue the components of the last dried bouquet individually around the bow, using longer stems behind the bow and shorter stems among the loops.

4   Tuck and glue a bow tail down each side of the arch. Cut the rose stems to 2"–2½" long. Glue one rose above and one below the bow and four roses evenly spaced along each side of the arch as shown in the large photo.

SPRING MAGNOLIA WREATH

18" round grapevine wreath
4 yards of 2⅝" wide pink/sage green wire-edged tapestry ribbon
6 oz. of dusty green preserved eucalyptus
1 stem of ivory silk magnolias with four 5"–8" wide blossoms, a bud and many leaves
3 stems of peach silk dogwood, each with five 2" wide blossoms and leaves
2 stems of yellow silk wildflowers, each with 9 sprigs of three 1½" wide blossoms
2 stems of blue silk forget-me-nots, each with 9 sprigs of four 1" wide blossoms
1 oz. of preserved light green tree fern
1 oz. of pink dried starflowers
24-gauge wire
low temperature glue gun and sticks

1 Cut the binding off the wreath and pull the wreath apart. Separate and position the vines to make three overlapping wreaths; wire to secure. Cut eucalyptus stems to these lengths: six 18", two 12" and four 8". Set aside the remaining eucalyptus for step 3. Glue one 18" sprig to the top front of the wreath, curving down the right side. Glue an 18" sprig above and one below the first. Glue an 8" sprig above and below the outer sprigs. Glue a 12" sprig over the center 18" sprig. Repeat on the left side, leaving a 6" empty space at the center top.

2 Use the ribbon to make a puffy bow (see page 26) with a center loop, eight 4½" loops and 22" tails. Wire to the wreath top, then wrap one tails down each side. Shape the magnolia blossoms. Cut the two largest blossoms with 4" stems; glue one on each side of the bow. Cut the two smaller blossoms with 8" stems, one with the bud. Glue one on each side as shown to extend halfway between the bow and the tips of the eucalyptus.

3 Cut the tree fern into 5"–9" sprigs; glue them evenly spaced among the eucalyptus and bow loops. Cut the remaining eucalyptus into 4"–6" sprigs and glue evenly spaced around the bow. Cut each dogwood stem into five single blossoms, each with a 5" stem. Glue five on each side of the bow near the magnolia blossoms and five around the bow as shown.

4 Cut the wildflowers and forget-me-not into 3"–5" sprigs. Glue them evenly spaced among the flowers and the bow loops. Divide the starflowers into clusters of 4–10 blossoms; cut the stems to 4"–6" and glue evenly spaced throughout the entire design. Attach a wire loop hanger (see page 18) to the upper back.

WREATH BASKET

12" round vine wreath
9" round vine wreath
two 3" long pink mushroom
  birds
one 2" wide grass bird's nest
three ½" long speckled plastic
  eggs
4 strands of 48" long peach
  raffia
4 strands of 48" long raffia
¼ oz. of brown American
  Moss® excelsior
1 stem of artificial bittersweet
  with eleven ¾" wide
  red/orange/green berries
2 stems of light rust silk
  mums, each with one 3½"
  and one 2½" wide blossom
1 stem of green silk ivy with 3
  sprigs of 1½"–3" wide
  leaves
4 stems of dried wild avena
3"x2"x1½" block of floral
  foam for silks
24-gauge wire
U-shaped floral pins
low temperature glue gun and sticks

1 Cut the binding wire on the 12" wreath; cut and remove two 34" long vines from it (save the rest for another project). Lay the wreath flat. To form the handle, insert one vine from the other wreath into the outside edge. Bend it to the opposite side, arching it 10" above the wreath base. Repeat with the other vine, then cut the excess stem and wire both ends securely to the wreath. Glue small tufts of excelsior to cover the wired areas. Trim the foam, cover it with excelsior and wire to the wreath inside the left handle base.

2 Hold all the raffia together and wire at one end. Use your fingernail to shred it into thin strips. Glue one end of the bunch to the left handle base and wrap it spiral fashion around the handle, making wraps 1"–1½" apart. Wire the strands together at the right handle base and cut off excess raffia. Glue one end of the trimmed raffia tails to the base of the nest; wrap them around the nest rim, gluing the other ends into the nest center. Glue the eggs into the nest front and a bird to the back rim. Glue a U-pin to the bottom of the nest; insert into the foam center. Glue the remaining bird to the handle top.

3 Cut the bittersweet branch to 16". Insert the stem into the foam near the handle; bend it up the handle and wrap it around the center top. Cut each 3½" mum with a 2" stem and insert them side by side in front of the nest. Cut one 2½" mum into a 7" sprigs, the other to 11"; insert the 11" sprig behind the handle and the 7" sprig between the nest and handle. Cut the ivy stem to 16" and wire it across the wreath front from handle to handle.

4 Cut the avena into 3"–5" sprigs and glue evenly spaced among the ivy and mums.

IVY & WILD ROSES

12" round grapevine
    wreath
2½ yards of 1⅜" wide
    gold/wine/green
    tapestry ribbon
1 green silk ivy bush
    with two 24", three
    16" and two 11"
    branches of ¾"–1¾"
    wide leaves
2 stems of red silk
    wild roses, each with
    three 1½"–3" wide
    blossoms and a bud
4 silk raspberry picks,
    each with seven ⅝"
    wide green, red and
    burgundy berries and
    13 leaves
½ oz. of dried hill
    flowers
24-gauge wire
low temperature glue
    gun and sticks

1 Cut the wreath binding. Soak the wreath in water for 30 minutes. Pull the center of the wreath out and down, fanning the vines at right angles to the wreath back as shown. Wire securely in place. Let dry completely.

2 Cut the ivy branches off the bush. Wire a 24" branch to the lower left side extending up to the right top of the upright wreath section. Wire the stem of the other 24" branch at the lower left and curve it through the wreath center and around the right front of the lower section. Wire a 16" branch over each 24" branch. Glue the stem of the last 16" branch to the left inside bottom of the upright wreath and weave it up over the center section as shown.

3 Cut one rose stem to 20". Wire it over the upper 24" ivy branch. Cut the lowest rose from the other stem

and glue to the lower left of the upright section. Cut the rest of that stem to 16" and wire it extending from right to left over the front 24" ivy branch.

4 Glue one raspberry pick to the top of the upright section, one among the three roses on the left side and one at the lower left. Glue the last pick just right of the center front. Use the ribbon to make an oblong bow (see page 26) with a center loop, ten 1½"–3" loops, a 16" and a 12" tail. Wire the bow to the lower left, angled toward the back; weave the 16" tail up the left side and the 12" around the right side to the front. Hold 3–6 hill flowers together at varying heights; cut the stems 2"–6" long and glue in a cluster near a rose. Repeat for ten more clusters, gluing one near each rose or bud as shown in the large photo.

CEDAR CIRCLET

one 18" round lacquered grapevine
   wreath
one 9" round lacquered grapevine
   wreath
2 stems of burgundy latex raspberries,
   each with two 4" sections of five ¾"
   wide berries and 5 leaves
4 oz. of green preserved cedar
one 6"–7" wide dried sponge mushroom
two 2½" wide dried pomegranates
two 2"–2½" wide dried protea flats
two 2½" wide pine cone roses
five 1¾" long selignum cones on stems
1 oz. of dried shag moss
22-gauge wire
low temperature glue gun and sticks

1 Cut the binding from the 9" wreath and spread the vines into three overlapping circles. Wire to secure them. Wire them to the left front of the 18" wreath as shown.

2 Cut the cedar into 7"–10" sprigs and glue extending in both directions over the 18" wreath from the left center, forming a crescent. Glue the sponge mushroom to the center of the crescent and the pomegranates side by side over the mushroom base as shown.

3 Glue a pine cone rose on each side of the pomegranates. Cut each berry stem into two 5" sprigs of five berries. Glue one above and one below the pomegranates and one 4½" away on each side. Cut the selignum stems to 4" and glue as shown.

4 Cut the stems off the protea flats and glue one above the upper pine cone rose. Glue the other right of the raspberries below the lower pomegranate. Separate the moss into 1"–2" tufts and glue evenly spaced among the cones and berries. Attach a wire hanger (see page 18) to the top back.

one 12" round straw wreath
one 12" round grapevine wreath
1 stem of purple latex grapes with 4 clusters of many ½" grapes and twenty 1"–2" wide leaves
2 oz. of red preserved oak leaves
2 oz. of burgundy preserved spiral eucalyptus
1 oz. of green dried sphagnum moss
1 oz. of green dried dwarf's beard moss
2 oz. of gray preserved forest coral moss
22-gauge wire, U-shaped floral pin, low temperature glue gun and sticks

1 Cut the binding from the grapevine wreath and loosen the branches. Use 12"–18" vine lengths to make a cage-like frame over the straw wreath, gluing the ends of each vine length into the straw 10" apart and repeating around the wreath as shown. Attach a U-pin hanger (see page 18) to the upper back.

2 Cut the four grape clusters and all the leaves from the stem. Glue two clusters extending opposite directions at the 10:00 position. Glue one at 6:00 and one at 2:30. Glue the leaves evenly spaced around the grapes. Glue 1"–2" tufts of sphagnum moss around each cluster, sparsely covering the straw 4" in each direction.

3 Cut the eucalyptus into 6"–8" sprigs and glue two on each side of each grape cluster, extending along the straw wreath. Cut the oak leaves into 3" sprigs and glue evenly spaced around each cluster.

4 Separate the forest coral into 1" tufts and glue them evenly spaced among the grapes, leaves and eucalyptus. Separate the dwarf's beard moss into ½"x4" tufts. Glue them randomly to the framework of grapevines as shown.

Straw Wreaths

Straw wreaths always look great when used in autumn or harvest designs; the color of the straw works well with the fall tones found in both styles. But these wreath bases are much more versatile than that. Plus, they're inexpensive and accessible, since they're carried in nearly every craft store.

Because of the moderate price, completely covering the straw wreaths with material such as moss, excelsior, raffia or plant materials provides the possibility of many unique designs. Once covered, the focal point can be developed using silk and dried materials. The Excelsior Heart on page 74 shows a straw wreath being turned into a romantic design with the addition of the delicate excelsior tendrils, roses and baby's breath.

All the ivy, berries and dried flowers on the Ivy Berry Wreath on page 80 have changed a straw wreath into a garden piece. With the addition of pine sprigs, it could be used as a Christmas wreath. The look and feel of a full spring garden was achieved in A Bounty Of Blossoms on page 78. If a customized look is desired, the vibrant colors of the flowers in this wreath can easily be substituted with muted-colored flowers or with monochromatic shades of a single color.

Straw wreaths are a great bargain because of their versatility and low cost—and they're easy to use!

Excelsior Heart

one 16" wide straw heart wreath
4 oz. of light gray American Moss® excelsior
2 stems of mauve silk roses, each with four 2"
*   wide blossoms and 2 buds*
thirty 36" strands of raffia
2 oz. of preserved baby's breath
1 oz. of lavender dried Siberian statice
20–30 U-shaped floral pins.
low temperature glue gun and sticks

1 Pull the excelsior into a long rope and wrap it spiral-fashion around the heart, completely covering it; secure with U-pins. Attach a U-pin hanger (see page 18) to the top back.

2 Cut the baby's breath into 3"–4" sprigs. Save two for step 4; glue the rest evenly spaced along the left side of the wreath. Pin one rose stem in the center of the baby's breath. Cut the roses and buds off the other stem, each with a 2" stem. Glue two roses to the conceal the bottom of the first stem and one bud above the top rose. Save the remaining bud and two roses for step 4.

3 Knot two strands of raffia together at one end. Repeat to make two more double strands. Pin one to the upper left back of the heart and wrap as shown, making the wraps 3½" apart. When that strand runs out pin it at the back, attach the next and continue until you return to the starting point. Cut off any excess raffia. Hold the remaining strands together and make a raffia collar bow (see page 24) with 2½" loops and 2½" tails. Glue it to the upper right.

4 Hold the remaining raffia together and fold in half. Glue the fold to the lower bow center; bring the tails down to the lower left and pin in place, draping through the flowers as shown in the large photo. Glue the remaining roses to the bow center. Glue remaining baby's breath around the bow. Cut the statice into 3" sprigs; glue four among the upper roses and the rest among the lower roses.

Dogwood Crescent

one 12" round straw wreath
1 stem of white latex cherry blossoms with one 6"
    and one 12" branch, each with several 1" wide
    blossoms and buds
1 stem of white silk dogwood with five 2" wide
    blossoms
1 latex blackberry pick with twelve ½" berries
2 oz. of white preserved ti tree branches
4 oz. of dried poa grass
2 oz. of dried bromus secalinus grass
1 oz. of dried rice grass
1 oz. of dried papaver
U-shaped floral pins
low temperature glue gun and sticks

1 Cut the cherry blossom stem to 14"; glue and pin it to the wreath at the 7:00 position with the branches extending downward. Cut the poa grass into 2–4" sprigs and wire in clusters of five. Cut the grassy poa stems into 5" sprigs and wire in clusters of five. Repeat for the bromus secalinus. Cut the ti tree into 5"–6" sprigs.

2 Glue the materials from step one to the left side of the wreath, starting at the center bottom and working upward to the center top. Gradually change the directions of the materials to extend upward as you get to 11:00. Alternate the varieties and the directions from inside to outside. Keep the inner sprigs fairly even with the line of the wreath and let the outer sprigs extend 4"–5" beyond the line of the wreath.

3 Cut the dogwood blossoms into five 2" sprigs. Glue three in a triangle 1½" apart at the top. Glue one to the center bottom and the other at 8:00. Cut the papaver into 2" sprigs and glue in a long cluster among the three top dogwood blossoms.

4 Cut the binding on the blackberry pick and separate it into pairs of berries. Glue three around the top dogwood blossoms and three every 4" cascading down the crescent. Cut the rice grass into 4" sprigs and glue evenly spaced throughout the crescent. Attach a U-pin hanger (see page 18) to the top back.

Wheat Bouquet Wreath

one 14" round straw wreath
1 stem of green latex rose leaves with four
    2"–6" sprigs of 2–3" long leaves
1 stem of white latex cherry blossoms with one
    6" and one 12" branch, each with several
    1" blossoms and buds
5 oz. of dried bearded wheat or barley
2 oz. of dried caspia
2 stems of dark pink dried peonies
1 oz. of dried buck or birch twigs
2 oz. of white dried floral buttons
two 2"–2½" wide pine cones
U-shaped floral pins
low temperature glue gun and sticks

1 Hold all the wheat together just under the heads. By pulling the back heads upward, arrange them to form a 10"x20" oval. Wire just below the lowest heads. U-pin the bouquet to the wreath as shown, inserting the pins through the back stems of the bouquet so they are out of sight.

2 Cut the rose leaves into two 6" long 6-leaf sprigs and three 2" long 2-leaf sprigs. Glue the 6" sprigs end to end extending outward from the wired area of the bouquet. Glue the 2" sprigs extending outward in a triangle over the ends of the 6" sprigs. Cut the stems off the peonies and glue them horizontally over the wire. Cut the cherry blossom stem into one 9" and one 5" sprig. Glue the 9" sprig left of the peonies curving upward. Glue the 5" branch right of the peonies angled downward. Glue a pine cone over the stem of each branch.

3 Make two clusters of floral buttons, each of fifteen blossoms with 1"–1½" stems. Wire each cluster at the bottom, then glue one above and one below the peonies, angled as shown. Make four clusters of four floral buttons with 4" stems; glue one on each side of each pine cone, angled in the same directions as the cherry blossoms.

4 Cut the caspia into ten 4–6" sprigs and glue evenly spaced around the flowers. Cut the twigs into ten 4–10" lengths and glue evenly spaced throughout the floral area with longer twigs in back and shorter ones around the peonies in front. Attach a U-pin hanger (see page 18) on the upper back.

Raffia & Gladiolus Wreath

one 16" round straw wreath
14–16 oz. of raffia
2½ yards of 2½" wide pink/ burgundy/
lavender/green printed ribbon
2 stems of pink silk gladiolus, each with five
2" and two 1" wide blossoms and 2 buds
1 stem of green silk ivy with 4 sprigs, 2 with
2 and 2 with four 2–3" long leaves
2 stems of burgundy silk roses, each with
three 1½" wide blossoms and 1 bud
2 oz. of green preserved ming fern
2 oz. of white dried ti tree branches
1 oz. of dried birch or buck twigs
about 60 U-shaped floral pins
24-gauge wire
tacky craft glue
low temperature glue gun and sticks

1 Use your thumbnail to shred the raffia into fine strands. To make a loop set, cut 25 strands to 10". Fold them in half and wire all the ends together. Repeat to make 60 loop sets, reserving 20 strands for step 2. Begin at the center bottom and use U-pins dipped in tacky glue to attach the loops to the wreath, angling them toward the center bottom. Completely cover the wreath front and sides. Attach a U-pin hanger (see page 18) to the top back.

2 Use the ribbon to make an oblong bow (see page 26) with a center loop, four 4" loops, two 6" loops and 14" tails. Glue to the center top. Loop a tail to each side and glue at the inside of the wreath. Use the reserved raffia to make eight more loop sets, four with 8" strands (4" loops) and four with 16" strands (8" loops). Glue the 4" loops among the bow loops and the 8" loops evenly spaced behind

the bow. Cut twenty-five 12"–14" raffia lengths and glue extending from beneath the bow for tails.

3 Cut each gladiolus stem to 18". Glue one on each side of the bow curving down the wreath. Cut each rose with a 3" stem and glue four to each side of the wreath among the gladiolus as shown. Cut the ivy into four 5" sprigs. Glue one on each side of the bow and one just inside the lower end of each gladiolus stem as shown.

4 Cut the ming fern into 5" sprigs and the ti tree into 6–8" sprigs. Glue them evenly spaced among the floral materials following similar angles. Cut fifteen 5–8" twig sprigs and glue them evenly spaced around the bow and among the bow loops and fern sprigs.

A Bounty of Blossoms

one 16" round straw wreath
2 stems of burgundy silk dahlias, each with one
    5" and one 2" wide blossom
2 stems of burgundy silk asters, each with five
    1–2" wide blossoms
3 stems of purple silk iris, each with one 5"
    long blossom
1 stem of blue silk asters with four 1½" wide
    blossoms
2 stems of white silk Queen Anne's lace, each
    with two 4" wide blossom heads
2 stems of white silk Queen Anne's lace, each
    with thirteen 2" wide blossom heads
2 oz. of dark green preserved salal leaves
4 oz. of dark green preserved spiral eucalyptus
2 oz. of dark blue dried larkspur
2 oz. of dried rice grass
3 oz. of green sphagnum moss
low temperature glue gun and sticks

Queen Anne's lace heads with 2" stems and glue evenly spaced among the flowers.

1 Cut the individual salal leaves from the branches and glue evenly spaced counter-clockwise around the wreath. Glue the moss to cover the open areas. Cut the eucalyptus into 3"–5" sprigs and insert through the moss into the wreath, spacing them fairly evenly on the wreath front, around the inside and the outside.

2 Cut the dahlias with 3" stems. Glue the large blossoms to the wreath at the 10:00 and 3:30 positions. Glue the small blossoms at 12:30 and 6:00. Cut the iris stems to 1" and glue to the wreath in a triangle as shown. Cut the burgundy asters with 2" stems and glue evenly spaced around the wreath; repeat with the blue asters.

3 Cut the 4" Queen Anne's lace heads with 3" stems and glue evenly spaced near the dahlias and irises. Cut the 2"

4 Cut the larkspur into 4" sprigs, divide into six clusters and glue the clusters evenly spaced among the previous flowers, angled counter-clockwise. Cut the rice grass into 2" sprigs and glue in clusters evenly spaced among all the materials. Attach a U-pin hanger (see page 18) to the top back.

Witch & Bittersweet

one 16" round straw wreath
one 20" long abaca witch on a broom
12 stems of dried wheat or barley
1 oz. of dried buck or birch twigs
2 stems of red/orange latex bittersweet, each
   with one 12" and one 15" branch of many
   ¾" wide berries
2 oz. of brown preserved oak leaves
1 pick with a 1" orange pumpkin
24-gauge wire, two U-shaped floral pins
low temperature glue gun and sticks

1 Hold the wreath in both hands and gently squeeze the sides to form an oval. Wire the witch's hat and broom securely to the wreath as shown. Glue the pumpkin pick just right of the witch's skirt.

2 Cut one bittersweet stem into one 13", one 5" and one 10" sprig. Cut the other stem into one 10" and three 5" sprigs. Glue the 5" sprigs evenly spaced around the pumpkin. Glue the two 10" sprigs and one 13" sprig behind the witch angling upward. U-pin the upper end of the 13" sprig to the wreath to secure.

3 Cut the twigs into eight 8–10" sprigs and three 5" sprigs. Glue the 5" sprigs evenly spaced around the pumpkin and the 8–10" sprigs evenly spaced among the bittersweet behind the witch.

4 Cut the stems off the wheat. Glue six wheat heads among the bittersweet vines and pumpkin right of the witch. Glue the remaining six heads evenly spaced among the bittersweet behind the witch. Cut the oak leaves into eight sprigs with 2" stems and glue evenly spaced throughout the floral area as shown above. Make a U-pin hanger (see page 18) on the top back.

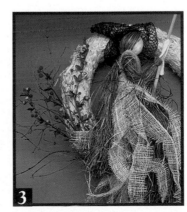

Ivy Berry Wreath

one 16" round straw wreath
2 yards of 2½" wide beige sheer wire-edged ribbon with a silver swirl pattern
1 green silk English ivy bush with seventeen 6"–10" branches of many 1"–2" leaves
1 green silk geranium ivy bush with nine 12"–18" branches of many 1"–2½" leaves
3 stems of red latex raspberries, each with two 4" sprigs of five ½" wide berries and four 3" sprigs of 3 leaves
2 stems of burgundy latex berries, each with seven 4" sprigs of five ⅜" wide berries
3 oz. of green dried sphagnum moss
3 oz. of green preserved plumosus
2 oz. of dried caspia
2 oz, of white preserved ti tree branches
30–40 U-shaped floral pins
30-gauge wire
low temperature glue gun and sticks

1 Cover the wreath with the moss, working from inside to outside and securing with the U-pins. Cut both ivy bushes into 5" sprigs and glue them to evenly cover the wreath, alternating the types.

2 Cut the plumosus into 5"–7" sprigs and glue them evenly spaced among the ivy sprigs extending in varied directions to create a "wild" look. Cover any large areas where the moss shows through.

3 Cut the raspberries and leaves into 4" sprigs and glue them evenly spaced around the wreath angled counterclockwise. Repeat with the burgundy berries. Cut thirty 4" sprigs of caspia and glue evenly spaced among the berries. Cut the ti tree branches into ten 6" sprigs and glue evenly spaced throughout the floral area, extending counterclockwise inside and outside the wreath.

4 Use the ribbon to make an oblong bow (see page 26) with a center loop, four 3½" loops, two 4" loops and 8" tails. Pin and glue the bow to the center bottom. Attach a U-pin hanger (see page 18) to the top back.

Harvest Bounty

This versatile wreath can be hung on the wall, too! Just add a hanger (see page 18) to the back.

one 12" round straw wreath
two 2½" wide purple latex plums, one 3" wide red latex half apple
1 stem of red/green silk maple leaves with twenty-nine 2"–4" long leaves
1 stem of green latex grape leaves with nineteen 3" long leaves
2 stems of red/burgundy latex raspberries, each with seven 1" wide
    berries and eight 2"–3" long leaves

one 5" wide lotus pod
two 4" wide dried pomegranates
eleven 2"–2½" long pine cones
27 stems of dried papaver
2 oz. of dried wild oats
3 dried mehogni pods
1 dried sponge mushroom
1 oz. of green mood moss
one 3"x9" amber pillar candle
1 glass hurricane candleholder
low temperature glue gun and sticks

1 Cut the leaves off both maple and grape stems and glue evenly spaced around the wreath. Glue the lotus pod at the 12:00 position. Glue a pomegranate at 5:00 and one at 9:00. Cut the papaver stems to 3". Glue two on each side of the lotus pod and four below it. Glue a cluster of six at 4:00 and another at 8:30. Glue the last three in a triangle extending outward from 1:30.

2 Glue the garlic at 3:00 with a plum just below and right of it. Glue the other plum at 10:30. Glue two mehogni pods at 3:00 and one behind the pomegranate at 9:00, extending out and downward.

3 Cut the berries and leaves apart with 1" stems. Glue three groups of two berries on the left side and two groups of four on the right side of the wreath. Glue the leaves evenly spaced around the wreath. Glue the mushroom left of the lower pomegranate. Glue the apple at 3:00, tucking it behind the mehogni pods.

4 Glue the pine cones around the wreath to fill any empty spaces. Glue moss to cover any wreath base that is still visible. Cut the wild oats into 6" sprigs and glue in clusters of three evenly spaced around the wreath. Insert the candle into the hurricane and set it inside the wreath.

Twig Wreaths

The introduction of twigs into floral design has changed the look and feeling of many decorating styles. Designs created with raffia, dried flowers, pods, cones and fruit, preserved greens, and natural-looking silk flowers all look wonderful when twigs are added. And, because of the naturalness of the resulting piece, it can be incorporated easily into nearly any decorating theme.

Along with garden and traditional, a home decorated in a romantic style can be enhanced with floral pieces constructed on twig bases such as flat wreaths or wreaths with woven lattice backs.

Twigs and branches are also perfect for achieving a woodsy or timberline floral look. Adding ferns, moss, cones and mushrooms to a twiggy wreath results in a stunning design—and it looks as though it was created from forest products gathered during an autumn walk. While collecting forest materials may be possible for some people, preserving them well enough to add to a wreath could be a problem. We're fortunate in that dried and preserved products, along with twig bundles and bases, can be found in craft stores, making it easy and convenient to create a one-of-a-kind wreath.

Whether as the base for a piece or as components added to the design, twigs and branches play an integral role in the 14 striking designs in this section. Twigs add a natural look and feeling to any design in which they're used—and it's easy to add them to wreaths since they look so great with so many components. They add freedom to designs with their lines and angles, as well as enhance the realism of each piece. The twig bases available in craft stores nearly design themselves by their shapes. Adding silk flowers, dried materials and ribbon following the lines already established can result in a beautiful piece in a matter of minutes.

If a wild look is desired for a wreath, simply add twigs to the outside of a regular vine wreath, angling them to extend one direction, following the lines of the wreath. Once they are glued or wired in place, construct the rest of the design by adding components.

Many twiggy bases can be found with artificial berries or silk ivy wired among the twigs. This provides a great start and simply requires adding components among the materials to achieve beautiful results. If you can't find the pieces with the berries or ivy in place, they can easily be added to a wreath by gluing or wiring in place before constructing the remainder of the design. Or, try a different look by gluing several different types, of berries in clusters among the twigs, mixing textures for added interest.

The design Chair In A Wreath on page 99 incorporates a small chair constructed from twigs into the wreath, then florals are added to make a clever and unique piece. If a less rustic look is desired, a white wicker chair can be substituted for a garden feel.

The garden look is achieved in the project on page 86, Roses & Ivy, by lightly painting the wreath base white. Coupled with the ivy and roses, the whitewashed wreath looks as though it were constructed fresh out of an English garden.

And wreaths aren't just for hanging on the wall. The Candle Centerpiece on page 88 features a twig wreath lying flat on the table with the design built around a hurricane candleholder. The wreath makes a very stable base, supporting the longer sprigs of spruce and wild oats which extend out to the edge.

Twig bases are very versatile while lending a wild or natural air to any design, as do twigs which are incorporated into a finished wreath. Twigs are almost magic when included in floral designing: Thin and fine twigs add a delicacy to designs while chunky branches can provide stability and strong lines. The more twigs added to a design the more natural or woodsy it will become. When a few are included, they become filler or line material in the design.

Because of their versatility, we've used twig bases in other sections of this book, including the Christmas and Take-Apart sections. Once we started playing with twigs and branches, there was no end to the ideas of their usage. Experiment with a bundle of birch or buck twigs from the craft store and discover how much fun they can be!

Roses & Ivy

22" wide TWIGS™ round open-weave wreath
1 green silk ivy bush with four 12", four 10" and four 8"
   branches of many 1"–2" wide leaves
3 stems of maroon silk roses, each with one 3½" wide
   blossom
3 stems of maroon silk rosebuds, each with 2 sprigs
   of three 1½" wide blossoms
1 stem of purple silk campanula with six 1½" wide blossoms
   and 7 buds
2 stems of white silk dogwood, each with five 2" wide
   blossoms
2 stems of lavender silk lilacs, each with two 9" sprigs of
   many blossoms
2⅔ yards of 2½" wide burgundy/lavender floral print ribbon
4"x4"x1" block of floral foam for silks
½ oz. of green sheet moss
24-gauge wire
green floral tape
white spray paint
low temperature glue gun and sticks

1 Lightly spray the wreath white. Cover the foam with moss and wire to the bottom front. Cut the ivy branches off the main stem. Insert a 12" branch into the left side of the foam and wire it to curve upwards. Wire a 12" branch above the first, tucking 3" of the stem behind the tip of the first. Insert two 12" branches into the right side, one curving up and one down. Insert a 10" branch on the left side curving down and a 10" branch between the two 12" branches on the right.

2 Use the ribbon to make a puffy bow (see page 26) with a center loop, six 4½" loops, a 12" and 14" tail. Glue it to the foam center. Insert 8" ivy branches around the bow. Cut one rose stem to 9" and insert above the bow extending upward. Cut the other rose stems to 7" and insert one above the bow extending forward and one below the bow.

3 Cut the rosebud stems into two 9", two 7" and two 5" sprigs. Insert both 9" sprigs between the two roses; insert a 7" and a 5" sprig just above the bow. Insert a 5" sprig in the bow center and a 7" sprig below the bow. Cut the campanula blossoms and buds off the main stem,

leaving 1" stems; floral tape each to a 7"–10" wire. Insert them evenly spaced among the roses and bow loops.

4 Cut each dogwood stem into five 6"–9" sprigs. Insert four sprigs above the bow, three among the bow loops and three below the bow, all near materials of similar lengths. Cut each lilac into two 7" sprigs. Insert two sprigs above the bow near the large roses. Insert two sprigs below the bow as shown in the large photo.

Mauve Teardrop

12"x18" TWIGS™ teardrop wreath
two 24" purple latex silk grape branches, each with 2 clusters of many ½" wide berries and many leaves
6 oz. of burgundy preserved eucalyptus
1 oz. of green preserved plumosus
1½ oz. of mauve dried starflowers
1 oz. of dried caspia
3⅔ yards of 5" wide burgundy twisted paper ribbon
24-gauge wire
low temperature glue gun and sticks

1 The wreath will hang with the pointed end up. Shape the grape branches and place one on the left front with the tip extending to the bottom; wire. Repeat with a branch on the right front with the tip extending 16" down the right side as shown.

2 Set aside four eucalyptus stems for use in step 3. Cut the remaining eucalyptus into 6"–10" sprigs. Glue the sprigs angled downward among the grape branches on both sides, using longer sprigs near the bottom and shorter sprigs near the top. Set one plumosus stem aside for use in step 3. Cut the remaining plumosus into 4"–6" sprigs and glue evenly spaced among the eucalyptus and grapes.

3 Untwist the paper ribbon and make an oblong bow (see page 26) with a center loop, ten 2½"–4" loops and 24" tails. Glue to the wreath top where the branches cross; weave a tail downward among the materials on each side. Cut the remaining eucalyptus and plumosus into 3"–6" sprigs; glue longer sprigs behind the bow loops and shorter sprigs among the loops as shown.

4 Hold 10–15 starflowers at varying heights and cut the stems 4" below the lowest blossom. Glue the cluster among the materials. Repeat with the remaining starflowers, gluing the clusters evenly spaced among all the materials. Cut the caspia into 3"–5" sprigs and glue evenly spaced throughout all materials, filling any empty spaces. Attach a wire loop hanger (see page 18) to the upper back.

Twig Wreaths - 87

Candle Centerpiece

16" round TWIGS™ open-weave wreath
9" tall hurricane candle holder with area
  for foam
8" peach taper candle
2 bird/pine picks, each with a 2" bird, a
  cone, a 1½" almond, 3 pods, 3 pine
  sprigs, 6 holly leaves
5 white pearl grape picks, each with a 7"
  section of ⅜"–½" grapes
4 stems of peach dried-look silk rosebuds,
  each with a 1½" long bud and two 3-
  leaf sprigs
two 2" long pine cones on picks
two 2" wide dried pomegranates on picks
14 oz. of green preserved black spruce
2 oz. of dried christina grass
1"x4"x4" block of floral foam for silks
30-gauge wire
low temperature glue gun and sticks

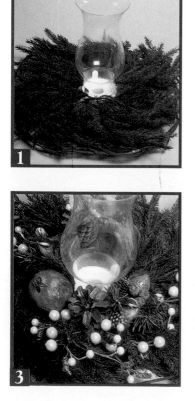

1 Cut the foam into two 1"x2"x4" blocks. Notch one side of each to fit around the hurricane base and glue in place. Cut twelve 11"–12" spruce sprigs and wire to the wreath extending out from the center. Set the hurricane in the center. Cut 6"–8" spruce sprigs and insert around the foam extending the same direction as the wreath sprigs.

2 Cut the grape picks to 7½". Insert them evenly spaced around the foam, tucked among the spruce sprigs and curved to follow the angles of the spruce. Cut the bird pick stems to 2"; insert on opposite sides of the hurricane, tucking them among the spruce.

3 Cut the pomegranate and cone pick stems to 2". Insert a cone left of each bird, next to the hurricane. Insert a pomegranate left of each cone, filling the empty areas next to the hurricane.

4 Cut the rose stems to 4". Insert them evenly spaced around the hurricane, extending over the spruce. Cut the christina grass into 8"–10" sprigs. Insert them evenly spaced extending from among the spruce sprigs at the same angles. Insert the candle.

Fall Wreath

16" round TWIGS™ open-weave wreath
2 yards of 1½" wide rust/gold wire-edged ribbon
2 stems of light yellow silk hollyhocks, each with six
2"–2½" wide blossoms and leaves
2 stems of burgundy/orange latex leaves, each with
five 3"–4" wide leaves and 2 berry sprigs
1 latex fruit pick with a 3" long quarter apple, a 1½"
blackberry, six ½"–1¼" various fruits and 6
leaves
8 stems of dried bearded wheat or barley
30-gauge wire
low temperature glue gun and sticks

1 Cut the hollyhock stems to 15". Bend them to follow the curve of the inner wreath edge. Wire one to extend up each side from the center bottom.

2 Cut the leaf stems to 13". Wire one over each hollyhock stem, pulling flower sprigs forward among the leaves.

3 Use the ribbon to make a puffy bow (see page 26) with a center loop, six 2½"–3" loops, a 13" tail and a 15" tail. Knot each tail 2" from the end, then trim diagonally. Glue the bow to the center bottom. Cut the stems off the wheat; glue the heads evenly spaced among the flowers.

4 Cut the components off the fruit pick, each with a 1" stem. Glue the apple right of the bow and the blackberry above it to the left. Glue the three smallest berries in a cluster below the bow and the pomegranate above the bow center. Glue a berry on the left among the flowers; glue the plum on the right. Glue the leaves around the bow to fill empty spaces. Attach a wire loop hanger (see page 18) at the upper back.

Safflower & Eucalyptus

24" wide TWIGS™ stick
   wreath
4 stems of fall-colored latex
   silk grape foliage, each with
   five 3"–3½" wide leaves
   and two berry clusters of six
   ³⁄₁₆" berries
3 oz. of brown preserved
   eucalyptus
three 12" long preserved kiwi
   branches
3 oz. of dried safflower
6 curly protea pods on picks
1 oz. of dried bromus grass
1 oz. of dried rice grass
2 oz. of rust dried strawflower
24 -gauge wire
low temperature glue gun and
   sticks

1 Starting at the left center, wire a foliage stem to curve upward. Wire another extending from the tip of the previous one to the wreath top. Repeat with two more stems extending downward beyond the lower wreath edge.

2 Wire the kiwi branches evenly spaced among the grape foliage. Cut the eucalyptus into 7"–14" sprigs; glue the sprigs among the foliage, following similar angles. In the center, glue shorter sprigs extending forward.

3 Cut the protea pod stems to 6"; glue them 3"–4" apart evenly spaced among the foliage as shown in the large photo. Cut the safflower stems to 6"–12" and glue throughout the entire design near items of similar lengths and at the same angles.

4 Cut the strawflower stems to 5"–9". Glue evenly spaced near materials of similar lengths. Cut the rice grass and bromus grass into 4"–8" sprigs. Glue evenly spaced among the previous materials, positioning longer sprigs on the outside and shorter sprigs on the inside and front of the wreath. Attach a wire loop hanger (see page 18) to the back.

Berries & Greens

20" wide twig and berry wreath*
4 oz. of green preserved princess pine
4 oz. of green preserved leather fern
4 oz. of dried papaver (18–20 stems)
2 oz. of preserved floral buttons
8" of 24-gauge wire
low temperature glue gun and sticks

*   If not available, buy the berries and wreath separately and glue 7"–9" berry sprigs as shown in step 1.

1 Carefully bend the berry sprigs forward and out toward the twig ends to give the wreath a fuller, more dimensional look. Turn the wreath over and cut away 20–25 twigs, each 5"–6" long, and set aside for step 4.

2 Cut the pine into 4"–6" sprigs and glue evenly spaced among the berries, angled in the same directions.

3 Cut the fern into 5"–7" sprigs and glue among the pine and berries, filling most empty spaces. Be sure to glue sprigs around the outside and inside edges of the wreath.

4 Cut the papaver and floral buttons into 5"–6" sprigs. Glue twigs from step 1, papaver and floral buttons evenly spaced among the pine and ferns, angled forward. Attach a wire loop hanger (see page 18) on the top back.

Wild Rose Wreath

12" wide TWIGS™ ring wreath
1 stem of yellow silk wild trailing roses with four
  1½"–3" wide blossoms and many leaves
3 stems of mulberry silk vervain spray, each with three
  6" long sprigs
1 stem of white artificial wild daisies with two 13" long
  sprigs and a 15" long sprig, each with many ¾"
  wide blossoms
½ oz. of green preserved plumosus
three 48" strands of natural raffia
three 48" strands of burgundy raffia
24-gauge wire
low temperature glue gun and sticks

1 Cut the trailing rose stem ½" below the lowest blossom or leaf sprig. Bend the lowest leaf sprig and blossom downward away from the rest of the stem. Bend the stem to match the curve of the wreath twigs and wire securely as shown. Attach a wire hanger (see page 18) to the top back.

2 Cut the vervain into 6" long sprigs. Glue one sprig below and one on each side of the lowest rose blossom on the right; repeat for each of the two blossoms at the wreath top.

3 Cut the wild daisy into 4"–5" long sprigs; set four aside for step 4. Glue the remaining sprigs evenly spaced among the previous materials. Cut the plumosus into 3"–6" sprigs; set aside 4–5 short sprigs for step 4. Glue the rest throughout the design, using shorter sprigs near the bow area and longer sprigs near materials of similar lengths.

4 Hold all the raffia together and handle as one to make a loopy bow (see page 27) with two 3" loops, one 9" and one 12" tail. Glue the bow into the space between the upper rose blossoms; weave the 12" tails down among the materials on the right side. Glue the remaining daisy sprigs and plumosus around and among the bow loops.

Magnolias & Delphinium

24" wide TWIGS™ arch
14"x17" TWIGS™ oval wreath with a vine lattice back
2 stems of cream silk delphiniums, each with many 2"–2½" blossoms and buds
1 stem of ivory silk magnolias with four 5"–8" wide blossoms, a bud and many leaves
3 stems of cream silk spreading astilbe, each with seven 16" grass blades and three 10" sprigs, each with one 6" blossom section
1 oz. of green preserved sprengeri
3 oz. of raffia
green floral tape
24-gauge wire
low temperature glue gun and sticks or tacky craft glue

1 Wire the arch securely to the wreath top. Cut each magnolia off the stem and to 7" long. Wire a large magnolia just to each side of the arch center and a small magnolia between the large one and the end of the arch on each side. Cut extra leaves from the stem and glue at the bases of the magnolia blossoms. Attach a wire loop hanger (see page 18) to the wreath top.

2 Cut a 9" sprig from the tip of each delphinium stem; glue one on each side near the small magnolia with the tips extending to the arch ends. Cut the rest of the delphinium into 3-blossom sprigs. Set two aside for step 3. Floral tape 6" wire lengths to the stems of the remaining short sprigs and glue them evenly spaced among the other magnolias, leaves and delphiniums.

3 Divide the raffia into thirds. Use ⅔ to make a collar bow (see page 24) with 3½" loops and 12"–18" tails. Use the rest to make a collar bow with 2½" loops and 8" tails. Glue the large bow to the arch center and the small bow to the lower right wreath. Glue the longest tails from the upper bow behind the lower bow. Glue a delphinium sprig from step 2 on each side of the lower bow loops.

4 Cut the astilbe into 10" sprigs; cut one in half and glue half among the delphinium blossoms on each side of the lower bow. Glue four sprigs extending outward on each side near the large magnolia blossoms. Cut the grass blades off at the stems, divide into two bunches and glue one on each side among the astilbe sprigs. Cut the sprengeri into 2"–8" sprigs. Glue them evenly spaced among all the floral materials, using shorter sprigs in and around the bows and longer sprigs near materials of similar lengths.

Greenery & Roses

18" TWIGS™ ring wreath with five 12"–18" twig loops

3 yards of 2⅝" wide green/burgundy tapestry wire-edged ribbon

3¼ yards of ½" wide antique gold flat wired braid

1 stem of mauve silk rhododendrons with a 6" and a 4" wide blossom head and many leaves

1 stem of pale pink silk wild roses with three 2"–4" wide blossoms and many leaves

1 stem of deep purple latex pokeberries with 3 sprigs of many green and purple ¼"–⅜" wide berries and leaves

8 oz. of green preserved willow eucalyptus

5 dried jacaranda pods on stems

one 8" long strobus pine cone

1 oz. of green preserved isolepsis grass

12–15 stems of preserved unbearded wheat, barley or triticum

low temperature glue gun and sticks

1 Wire eucalyptus branches onto the wreath center top to extend down each side, farther on the left than on the right. Wire four isolepsis stems together 15" from the tips; cut off the bases. Make five more clusters and glue three on each side of the wreath between the branches.

2 Cut the large rose sprig off the main stem and to 6" long. Wire it to extend left from the center top. Cut the rest of the stem to 14" and glue it extending right. Cut the large rhododendron head to 5" long and wire it over the rose stem, angled right. Cut the small rhododendron head to 7" long and wire it to extend between the two roses on the right side.

3 Use the tapestry ribbon to make a puffy bow (see page 26) with a center loop, four 5" loops, a 25" and a 22" tail. Glue to the center top. Weave the longer tail among the twigs at the center bottom; loop and glue the shorter tail among the flowers on the right. Use the braid to make another puffy bow with a center loop, eight 3" loops, a 32" and a 26" tail. Glue it below the tapestry bow's center and loop the tails among the eucalyptus leaves, one on each side.

4 Cut the berry stem into one 3-sprig and one 2-sprig section, both 14" long. Wire the 3-sprig section on the right and the other on the left. Cut the jacaranda pods into 6"–10" lengths; glue three on the right and two on the left as shown. Glue the cone to extend from below the bow; glue any remaining rhododendron leaves around the bow. Cut the wheat into 6"–12" sprigs and glue evenly spaced among the flowers as shown in the large photo. Glue 8" isolepsis sprigs below the bows.

40" long TWIGS® swag
14"x11" TWIGS® oval wreath
3" wide straw bird's nest
2½ yards of 1½" wide bronze taffeta wire-edged ribbon
1 stem of burgundy latex grapes with a 9" section of many
⅝"–1" wide grapes and an 11" sprig of five 2"–4½" leaves
2 oz. of dried wild avena
1 oz. of green sheet moss
two 3" mauve/burgundy mushroom birds

2 stems of burgundy/orange silk fall leaves, each with five
3"–3½" long leaves and 2 berry clusters
two 29" long green/burgundy silk grape leaf branches, each with
four 6"–14" sprigs of 2"–4" leaves
3 stems of peach silk daisies, each with three 9"–10" sprigs of
three 1½" wide blossoms and leaves
24-gauge wire
low temperature glue gun and sticks

1 Wire the wreath to the swag center. Cut off the lowest 14" sprig from each grape leaf branch and set aside. Wire the branches to the swag extending 19" from the center toward each end. Wire two 14" sprigs end to end curving down the right side of the wreath. Wire the nest to the lower right.

2 Cut two 4" grape clusters; glue one on each side of the nest. Cut the rest of the grapes into two 6" clusters; glue one to extend down and right from the swag center and the other to extend up and left. Cut the remaining sprig of grape leaves into two 6" sprigs; glue one between the upper grapes and one below the rest. Cut each daisy stem to 16". Glue them to the swag with one extending toward each end. Cut the lowest 8" sprig off the last daisy stem and glue it to extend left from under the upper grapes. Cut the rest to 10" and glue to extend right from under the same grapes.

3 Cut each fall leaf stem to 13". Glue one to extend toward each swag end. Cut 54" of ribbon and knot 4"–5" from each end. Glue one knot near a swag end, then tuck and glue the ribbon among the materials to the other swag end. Repeat with the other ribbon length, but begin on the left side of the wreath and bring the ribbon down below the nest.

4 Cut the avena into 4"–14" sprigs and glue them evenly spaced near materials of similar lengths. Cut ten inconspicuous twigs from the swag back and glue among the avena. Glue eight to ten 1"–1½" moss tufts evenly spaced on the wreath and swag, then glue a bird to the swag center and one to the wreath as shown in the large photo. Attach a wire loop hanger (see page 18) to the back.

Oval Wreath

12"x16" TWIGS™ oval open-weave wreath
1 oz. of white dried German statice
10 stems of purple dried larkspur
1 oz. of green preserved mini holly
10 pink dried roses
2 oz. of mauve dried baby everlastings
low temperature glue gun and sticks

1 Cut the statice into 3" sprigs. Glue the sprigs extending from the center bottom up each side. Set aside any remaining sprigs for step 4.

2 Cut the holly into 3"–5" sprigs; glue them evenly spaced among the statice, extending upward on both sides. Cut the larkspur into 3"–7" sprigs. Glue them extending upward on each side from the center bottom with the shorter sprigs near the bottom and the longer sprigs extending to the top outer edge of the wreath.

3 Cut the roses to 3" and glue them spaced 2"–3" apart throughout the other materials, placing larger blossoms near the bottom and smaller blossoms on the sides.

4 Cut the everlastings into 3"–6" sprigs and glue them evenly spaced among the previous materials. Glue any remaining statice sprigs from step 1 to fill open spaces.

Wild Twigs Wreath

25" wide wild twig wreath*
2⅓ yards of 1½" wide brown/black/
 red/green tapestry wire-edged ribbon
2 green vinyl angel pine picks, each
 with 3 branches of 6–8 sprigs
2 brown/green/rust latex peach picks,
 each with a 2½" half peach, nine
 ⅜"–1" berries and fruit, and four
 2½"–4" leaves
2 oz. of green preserved ming fern
five 7"–9" dried chili peppers
five 2½"–4" pine cones
three 3" dried orange slices
4 oz. of dried canella
green florist tape
6" of 24-gauge wire
low temperature glue gun and sticks

*If not available, wire or glue curving
twigs to a grapevine wreath, extending
outward clockwise around the wreath.

1 Attach a wire hanger (see page 18) to the upper back. Cut each pine stem into three branches; set one aside for step 4. Glue the rest evenly spaced around the wreath, spreading them to extend among the twigs.

2 Remove the lower leaf from one peach pick. Cut each pick into two sprigs of fruit, then remove a berry each from two different sprigs and a plum from another sprig. Hold the separate pieces together with the leaf and wrap the stems with florist tape, making another sprig. Glue a fruit sprig over the stem of each pine sprig.

3 Cut the ming fern into 4"–6" sprigs. Glue them evenly spaced near and among the pine sprigs. Glue the peppers evenly spaced around the wreath, angling them between the pine sprigs. Break each orange slice in half and glue them around the wreath, spacing them equally. Loop the ribbon around the wreath, tucking it among the twigs and stems; glue it to hold.

4 Glue the cones equally spaced around the wreath. Cut the canella into 3"–3½" clusters and glue around the wreath, spacing them evenly on the inside and outside. Cut the sprigs off the pine branch from step 1 and glue to fill any empty spaces. Cut a few 12"–16" twigs from the back of the wreath. Glue to the front, extending forward over the previous materials.

Twig Wreaths - 97

Garden Heart Wreath

13" wide TWIGS™ sunburst
  heart wreath
2 stems of silk wild grapes, each
  with three sprigs of nine
  ³⁄₈"–⁵⁄₈" wide grapes and
  many leaves
2 latex apple/berry picks, each
  with a 2³⁄₄" quarter apple,
  seven ³⁄₈"–1¼" berries and
  fruits, and 6 leaves
2 burgundy latex pomegranate
  picks, each with three
  1¼"–1½" wide pomegranates
  and 3 leaves
2 stems of dark burgundy silk
  skimmia, each with three
  sprigs of 1½"–3" long
  blossom clusters and
  many leaves
10 stems of red dried roses
½ oz. of dried wild avena
24-gauge wire
low temperature glue gun and
  sticks

1 Bend a grape stem to follow the curve of one side of
the wreath; wire securely, then cut off any excess.
Repeat for the other side. Attach a wire loop hanger (see
page 18) to each side of the wreath top back.

2 Wire a pomegranate pick to the upper right, bending it
to follow the wreath. Wire an apple/berry pick halfway
down the right side. Repeat on the left side, placing the
apple/berry pick at the upper left and the pomegranate pick
midway down the left side. Cut each skimmia stem into 4"
sprigs. Glue a sprig over the stem of each pick and one
below the lower fruit as shown. Cut any extra leaf sprigs off
the stem and glue to fill any empty spaces.

3 Cut the avena into 2"–4" sprigs and glue evenly spaced
throughout the fruit and skimmia on each side.

4 Cut the rose stems to 4". Glue five on each side, evenly
spaced, alternating them to the inside and outside of
the picks as shown.

Chair on a Wreath

20"x28" TWIGS™ teardrop wreath
18" tall TWIGS™ chair
2 stems of yellow/pink latex roses, each with two 3" wide
blossoms, 3 buds and leaves
1 stem of pink latex peonies with one 3½" wide blossom, 1
bud and leaves
2 stems of gold-brushed latex apples and pomegranates, each
with a 2" burgundy pomegranate, a 1¼" red apple, two 1"
blackberries, ½" berries and leaves
1 gold-brushed latex peach/apple pick with a 2" peach quarter,
a 1½" burgundy apple, two 1" blackberries, various other
berries and leaves
1 green silk purple passion bush with eighteen 6"–11" branches
of 1½"–2½" long leaves
3 stems of green silk leatherleaf fern, each with five 4"–5"
sprigs
30-gauge wire
low temperature glue gun and sticks

1 Wire the chair to the wreath bottom angled right. Cut six 11" purple passion branches off the main stem. Wire four evenly spaced up the left side of the wreath, beginning at the lower left and extending up to the center top. Wire two 9" branches up the chair back on the left; wire two 6" branches to extend along the front seat edge.

2 Trim the yellow roses to 18". Wire one to extend up the left side of the wreath. Wire the other to the wreath bottom, extending right. Trim the peony to 12". Wire it to the lower left, positioning the blossom between the lowest rose blossoms.

3 Cut each pomegranate stem into two 5" sprigs. Glue one near the uppermost rose and one near the peony blossom. Glue a sprig below the peony and one between the two lowest roses, under the chair. Trim the peach stem to 7"; glue it to extend along the chair seat front.

4 Cut the remaining purple passion branches off the stem. Glue two 6" branches among the chair leaves; glue the rest evenly spaced among the flowers on the wreath. Cut the sprigs off the fern stems. Glue two among the leaves on the chair, then glue the rest evenly spaced among the flowers on the wreath. Attach a wire loop hanger (see page 18) to the back.

Styrofoam® Wreaths

*E*very craft store has an aisle just brimming with Styrofoam® forms; many are wreaths of different shapes and sizes. But what can you do with those? While they look pretty boring sitting in a pile on the shelf, they are a great beginning for creating some clever and beautiful floral designs. Those foam bases are inexpensive and easy to use, allowing products to be glued, pinned, wrapped or wired to them.

Many different styles and looks can be achieved by completely covering the foam base. The Magnolia & Grape Ivy Wreath on page 107 begins by covering the base with green paper ribbon to hide the white foam. Then dried and silk materials are pinned over the entire wreath, producing a fresh, garden look.

In contrast to that project, the Pods & Cinnamon design on page 108 and the Apple Harvest wreath on page 106 both begin with a wreath covered with moss—yet each achieves a different look, one woodsy and the other natural. Mixing the mosses brings in different textures and colors to the design, adding interest and excitement to the wreath. Both wreaths are similar, yet each has its own unique look.

Another twist within these pages is the Hearts In A Wreath on page 109. Two small Styrofoam® hearts are covered with shirred, wire-edged ribbon, then added to a feathery twig wreath, all to produce a wreath with romance.

Many techniques for covering and enhancing foam wreaths have been included within this section, and whatever style you're looking for can be produced with a foam base.

Raffia Wraps & Loops

10" round extruded foam wreath
5 oz. of mauve raffia
5 oz. of natural raffia
1 stem of green/burgundy silk grape leaves with 3
  sprigs of 2"–3½" wide leaves
2 stems of violet silk sweet peas, each with 2 sprigs
  of eight 1½"–2" blossoms, buds and leaves
1 stems of silk Queen Anne's lace, each with 12
  sprigs of many ⅜" wide blossom clusters
24-gauge wire
U-shaped floral pins
low temperature glue gun and sticks

back view

1 Hold 15 strands of natural raffia together and wire one end. Glue this end to the wreath back and wrap spiral fashion around the wreath with the wraps 1"–1½" apart. Add more strands as needed, gluing the ends in back. Repeat with mauve raffia, wrapping between the previous wraps to completely cover the foam and make a striped effect. Make 25 mauve and natural raffia loops (see page 27), each 3" long. Dip U-pins into glue and attach the loops equally spaced around the wreath back as shown. Glue a U-pin hanger (see page 18) to the top back.

2 Cut the grape leaf stem into one 10" and two 8" sprigs. Starting at the left center, pin one 8" sprig curving up the wreath front and the other curving down. Pin the 10" sprig to trail off the wreath bottom.

3 Cut the sweet pea into two 10" and two 8" sprigs. Insert a 10" sprig into the upper foliage so the sprig tips are even with the grape leaf tips, curving it downward. Insert an 8" sprig 2" below and left of the first sprig, curving it along the outer wreath edge. Insert the remaining sprigs curving down through the lower foliage as shown.

4 Use the remaining raffia to make a collar bow (see page 24) with 3" loops and 6"–12" tails; glue to the open area on the left side as shown. Cut the Queen Anne's lace into two 10", three 5" and four 3" sprigs. Glue each 10" sprig near a sweet pea sprig of similar length, two 5" sprigs above the bow and one 5" sprig below the bow. Insert the 3" sprigs

Potpourri Wreath

10" round extruded foam wreath

4 oz. of ivory/brown vanilla scented potpourri

3⅔ yards of 2⅜" wide gold mesh ribbon

1 gold/ivory silk magnolia pick with a 6½" and a 3½" wide blossom, many 1½"–2½" wide latex ivy leaves and four clusters of two to four ⅜"–¾" wide gold/brown berries

½ oz. of dried nigella

½ oz. of dried rice grass

24-gauge wire

tacky craft glue

low temperature glue gun and sticks

1 Spread tacky glue over the wreath front and sides. Press potpourri into the glue; let dry. Glue individual potpourri pieces to cover empty spaces, varying the colors.

2 Cut 3 yards of ribbon. Glue one end to the wreath back and wrap the wreath spiral fashion with the wraps slightly overlapping, enclosing the potpourri; glue the ribbon end over the first end. Glue a wire loop hanger (see page 18) to the top back.

3 Bend the 6½" magnolia blossom with its foliage and berries downward over the stem opposite the 3½" magnolia, foliage and berries. Cut the stem to 2" and wire it securely to the left center of the wreath. Use the remaining ribbon to make a puffy bow (see page 26) with a center loop and eight 3½" loops. Glue the bow between the magnolias.

4 Cut the nigella into 3"–5" sprigs; glue evenly spaced among the magnolias and bow loops, using larger heads near the bow and smaller ones near the ends of the design area, following similar angles. Cut the rice grass into 4"–6" sprigs; glue evenly spaced among all the previous materials.

Ribbon-Wrapped Wreath

12" round Styrofoam® wreath
9 yards of 4" wide maroon twisted paper ribbon
1 stem of peach silk dogwood with five 4" wide blossoms, buds and many leaves
7 stems of pink/burgundy silk roses, each with two 1½" wide roses and a bud
1 oz. of green preserved sprengeri
½ oz. of maroon dried German statice
½ oz. of dried brisa maxima
4"x1½"x1½" block of floral foam for drieds
½ oz. of green sheet moss
U-shaped floral pins
24-gauge wire
low temperature glue gun and sticks

1 Untwist all the paper ribbon. Cut a 1-yard length and set aside for step 2. Cut the rest in half and hold the ends together; pin and glue to the wreath back. (A) Wrap both lengths through the wreath and over the front. Pull ribbon 2 from behind ribbon 1 and wrap it to the right, around the back and over the front. (B) Cross ribbon 1 to the right over ribbon 2. Wrap it around the back of the wreath and over the front. Cross ribbon 2 to the right over ribbon 1 and wrap as before. Repeat around the wreath; pin and glue the ends at the back. Glue a U-pin hanger (see page 18) to the top back.

2 Cut a 10" ribbon length and set it aside. Use the remaining ribbon to make a flat bow (see page 25) with a 2" center loop, two 5", two 4" and two 3" loops. Place the bow on the lower wreath front. Insert the 10" length through the center loop and wrap the ends to the back. Pin and glue to secure.

3 Trim the floral foam to fit inside the wreath bottom; glue it in place. Pin moss to cover the foam. Cut the dogwood sprigs to these lengths: one 9", one 7", one 5", one 4" and one 2". Insert the 9" sprig at the back center of the foam, then insert the 7" sprig in front and to the left of it. Insert the 5" sprig to the right of the 7" sprig, the 4" below left, and the 2" sprig above and right of the bow center. Cut the sprengeri into 2"–10" sprigs and insert near dogwood blossoms of similar lengths. Cut the rose stems to 6" and glue evenly spaced throughout the design. Cut 3"–9" sprigs of German statice and brisa maxima; insert them near materials of similar lengths.

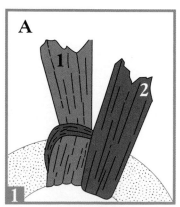

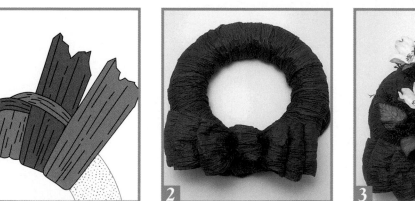

12" round Styrofoam® wreath
3 yards of dark green twisted paper ribbon
12 oz. of dark green preserved eucalyptus
12 stems of dark red dried roses with leaves
10 stems of dried white larkspur, 2 oz. of preserved baby's breath
2⅔ yards of 2½" wide burgundy organza ribbon with gold wired edges
U-shaped floral pins, 24-gauge wire, low temperature glue gun and sticks

1 Untwist the paper ribbon. Pin one end to the wreath back, then wrap spiral fashion to completely cover the wreath; pin the end over the first end. Cut the eucalyptus into 6"–8" sprigs; hold three sprigs together and pin to the wreath front extending clockwise. Continue around the wreath, positioning the tips of each bunch over the stems of the last, entirely covering the wreath front, inner and outer edges. Attach a U-pin hanger (see page 18) to the top back.

2 Use the organza ribbon to make a puffy bow (see page 26) with a center loop, six 2½" loops, and one 40" tail. Glue the bow to the center top and trail the tail around the wreath front, tucking it into the eucalyptus in four evenly spaced places; glue the end behind the bow loops. Cut the baby's breath into 3"–4" sprigs; glue them evenly spaced throughout the eucalyptus, with four sprigs among the bow loops.

3 Cut the larkspur into 4"–6" sprigs. Glue them evenly spaced around the wreath front. Use shorter sprigs near the wreath center and longer sprigs on the outer edge. Glue four 4" sprigs among the bow loops.

4 Cut the roses to 3". Glue them 3"–4" apart among the eucalyptus and larkspur, alternating them on each side of the ribbon. Glue a single rose near the bow center, then glue two leaves near each rose.

Apple Harvest

16" round Styrofoam® wreath
6 oz. of natural sheet moss
1 burgundy/green silk apple/grape swag
    with 2 sprigs of six 1½"–2¼"
    apples, 2 clusters of ⅝" grapes,
    many leaves, twigs and grass sprigs
two 3"–4" wide dried lotus pods
ten 4"–6" long dried chili peppers
4 oz. of brown preserved eucalyptus
2 oz. of dried bloom broom
2⅔ yards of 1½" wide brown/green fall
    print ribbon
U-shaped floral pins
24-gauge wire
low temperature glue gun and sticks

1 Cover the wreath sides and front with moss; secure with U-pins. Attach a wire loop hanger (see page 18) to the top back.

2 Cut the apple swag into two equal sections. Wire one to curve from the center top down each side, leaving an 8" opening at the wreath bottom.

3 Make an oblong bow (see page 26) with a center loop, ten 2"–3" loops and 16" tails; glue it into the open space. Weave one tail among the apples on each side. Insert a lotus pod above the bow on the right and another below the bow on the left.

4 Glue the peppers evenly spaced throughout the materials. Cut the eucalyptus and bloom broom into 3"–5" sprigs. Glue them evenly spaced among the apples and bow loops around the inner and outer wreath edges, filling empty spaces.

Magnolia & Grape Ivy

18" round Styrofoam® wreath
6 yards of green twisted paper ribbon, untwisted
3⅛ yards of 3" wide burgundy wire-edged ribbon with a green sheen
1 burgundy silk magnolia with an 8" wide blossom and 5 leaves
1 stem of burgundy silk plumosus with 3 branches of 9 pellet-covered blossom sprigs and 4 leaves
1 green/rust/burgundy silk grape ivy bush with a 34", a 28", two 19" and three 11" branches of 1"–2" wide leaves
1 stem of salmon silk field grass with twenty-five to thirty 7"–9" long blades
1 stem of mauve artificial raspberries with ten ¾" wide raspberries and many 1¼" wide silk leaves
4 oz. of dark green preserved plumosus
8 oz. of medium green preserved ming fern
1 oz. of green sheet moss
antique walnut spray stain
8" of 24-gauge wire, U-shaped floral pins
low temperature glue gun and sticks

1 Use the paper ribbon to wrap the wreath spiral-fashion, completely covering it; glue the ends. Cut the ming fern into 8"–10" sprigs. Attach to the wreath with U-pins, applying glue to the ends before inserting. Angle the sprigs counter-clockwise around the front and sides, sparsely covering it.

2 Cut the ivy branches off the main stem. Pin the 34" and 19" branches around the outer edge of the wreath. Pin the 28" and an 11" branch around the front of the wreath. Cut the last two 11" branches into six 5" sprigs. Pin them evenly spaced around the inner wreath edge and to fill any empty spaces.

3 Cut the preserved plumosus into 6"–10" sprigs. Glue them evenly spaced among the ming and ivy sprigs at similar angles. Lightly spray the silk plumosus and the

magnolia with stain; let dry. Cut the magnolia to 9" and bend the flower forward. Pin the flower to the wreath just left of center top; shape the leaves and petals.

4 Use the ribbon to make an oblong bow (see page 26) with a center loop, eight 3"–5" loops and one 28" tail. Pin it to the wreath just right of the magnolia. Loop and glue the tail down the right side of the wreath. Cut the silk plumosus into one 8" and two 9" sprigs. Glue the 8" sprig angled to the right and the 9" sprigs angled down the left side of the wreath as shown. Cut the berry stem into two 6" sprigs; glue both to extend left of the magnolia as shown. Cut the field grass stem to 9"; glue extending left from under the magnolia. Attach a U-pin hanger (see page 18) to the back (see page 18).

Pods & Cinnamon

12" round Styrofoam® wreath
4 oz. of green sheet or sphagnum moss
2 oz. of dwarf's beard moss
2 oz. of Spanish moss
2 yards of 1⅜" wide brown burlap
  wire-edged ribbon
two 18" long cinnamon sticks
assorted pine cones (fourteen 1½"–2"
  tall cones were used here)
2 oz. of ¼"–½" long buckbrush cones
  on stems
pods on picks: two 2½" long fiber ball
  pods, two 2¾" wide curly proteas,
  one 3" long mehogni pod, one 5½"
  long okra pod, one 2" wide bell pod
2 oz. of dried canella
8" of 24-gauge wire
U-shaped floral pins
low temperature glue gun and sticks

1 Cover the wreath front with sheet moss, securing it with U-pins. Pull off 3"–4" long tufts of dwarf's beard moss and tuck them evenly spaced throughout the green moss, securing with pins. Repeat with Spanish moss, spacing these tufts evenly throughout the previous mosses.

2 Use the ribbon to make an oblong bow (see page 26) with a center loop, four 2½" loops, two 3½" loops, a 14" and an 8" tail. Pin it to the wreath front at the right center. Use wire cutters to cut the picks or stems of all the pods to 2". Insert a protea and a fiber ball pod into the wreath above the bow as shown. Insert the okra to angle up the wreath above the protea.

3 Insert the bell pod into the foam just below the bow, angled left; glue a 2" cone angled right as shown. Insert a fiber ball pod below the bell pod, a protea to its right and the mehogni below right of it. Glue the rest of the cones evenly spaced, above and below and angled away from the bow, using larger ones near the bow and smaller ones to the outside.

4 Break each cinnamon stick into three 3"–4" sticks. Glue them into the foam among and around the previous components at similar angles. Cut the canella into 4"–6" sprigs. Glue them evenly spaced among all the components. Cut the buckbrush cone sprigs to 2"–3" and glue evenly spaced to fill any empty areas; also use moss tufts to fill spaces among the cones and pods. Tuck and glue the 14" ribbon tail down through the center of the lower components and the 8" tail along the lower right side of the wreath. Attach a U-pin hanger (see page 18) to the upper back.

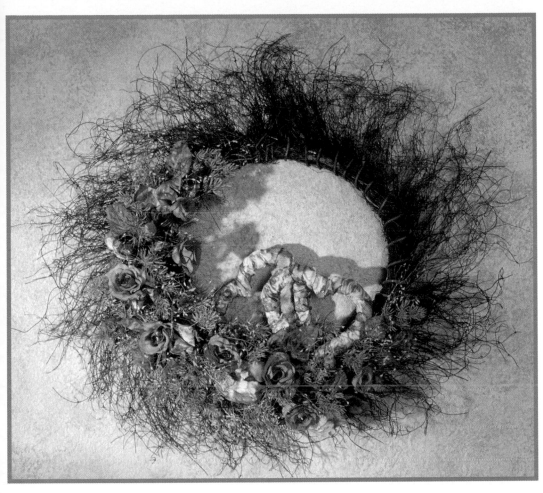

Hearts in a Wreath

24" round sunburst root wreath
two 6" extruded foam heart wreaths
2⅓ yards of 2½" wide mauve/ sage green/gold wire-edged ribbon
2 stems of mauve silk roses, each with one 1¼" and three 2" wide blossoms, 2 buds and many leaves
2 stems of green latex rose leaves, each with a 13" section of twenty 2"–3" long leaves
2 oz. of sage green preserved ming fern
1 oz. of dried rice grass
needlenose pliers
24-gauge wire
low temperature glue gun and sticks

1 Hold the root wreath at the top and bottom and gently push them together, forming an oval—be careful not to break the roots. Snip 20–25 roots from the back, being careful not to make any empty spaces in the wreath. Set these roots aside for step 4.

2 Cut a 24" ribbon length; use the pliers to gently pull the wires while gathering the ribbon from each end. Gather one side more tightly than the other. Place one end of the ribbon at the bottom point of a heart wreath, with the more tightly gathered edge to the inside. Glue the edges at the back, working around the wreath and fitting the ribbon to the heart. (The edges will not meet at the back, but make sure they do not show from the front.) Completely cover the heart front, then repeat for the other heart. Wire the hearts to the center bottom of the root wreath, angled as shown.

3 Cut each rose leaf stem to 13". Wire one to the wreath front curving up the left side from 7:00 to 10:00. Wire the second to extend right from 7:00 to the 4:00 position. Cut each rose stem to 12". Wire one over each leaf stem, curving as for the leaves and extending to within 1" of the leaf ends. Tuck and glue the remaining ribbon to loop through the design from 5:00 to 11:00.

4 Cut five 2"–3" fern sprigs and glue them at the 7:00 position, extending forward. Cut the remaining fern into 3"–5" sprigs. Cut the rice grass into 3"–4" sprigs. Glue the root sprigs from step 1, the fern and the rice grass sprigs evenly spaced among all the materials, extending at similar angles. Attach a wire loop hanger (see page 18) to the upper back.

White Rose Centerpiece

one 12" round extruded foam wreath
3 stems of white silk roses, each with a 3½" wide rose
  and 2 leaves
1 stem of burgundy silk carnations with five 2" wide
  blossoms
2 stems of lavender latex freesias, each with two 10" long
  sections of two to three 3" wide blossoms and buds
1 green silk English ivy bush with eighteen 5"–14" branches
  of many 1"–2" wide leaves
2 oz. of preserved baby's breath
3 oz. of burgundy preserved baby eucalyptus
about 30 U-shaped floral pins
ten 2" long wired wood picks
burgundy taper candles: one 12", one 10", one 8" tall
3 green plastic candle cups
antique walnut spray stain
low temperature glue gun and sticks

1 Wrap excelsior around the wreath, securing it with U-pins to completely cover the wreath. Insert the candle cups 1" apart at one side of the wreath. Cut the ivy bush into 18 branches and pin them into the foam, covering the wreath from inside to outside. Leave two long sprigs loose to drape onto the table in front.

2 Hold the roses at arm's length and lightly mist them with the antique spray. Cut the rose stems to 2", 3" and 3½". Insert the 3½" rose just right of the candle cups, the 3" rose 3" to the left of the candle cups and the 2" rose 8" left of the candle cups, all angled away from the cups.

3 Cut the carnation stems to 3". Glue them evenly spaced among the roses as shown. Cut each freesia into two sprigs, each with 3" stems. Glue two on each side of the wreath extending horizontally as shown, inserting the glued end deep into the excelsior.

4 Cut seven 4"–6" eucalyptus sprigs and insert evenly spaced around the candle cups as shown. Cut the remaining eucalyptus into 3"–5" sprigs and wire to wood picks in clusters of three. Insert evenly spaced among the flowers. Cut the baby's breath into fifteen 3"–5" sprigs and insert evenly spaced among the flowers with longer sprigs toward the back. Insert the candles into the cups as shown in the large photo.

one 12" round extruded foam wreath
one 8"x4" round bleached willow basket with an 11" tall handle
2½ yards of 1" wide light yellow iridescent organdy wire-edged ribbon
2 burgundy silk rose picks, each with three 2" wide roses
2 oz. of green dried sphagnum moss
6 oz. of dried caspia
2 oz. of dark blue dried larkspur
2 oz. of burgundy preserved hill flowers
2 oz. of dried nigella
2 oz. of dried brisa media
1 oz. of green preserved plumosus
22-gauge wire, low temperature glue gun and sticks

1 Spread glue over a small area of the wreath and press moss into the glue; repeat to cover the entire wreath. Push the wreath down over the basket handle to rest on the basket rim. Cut the caspia into 3" sprigs and glue them to the wreath angled counterclockwise to cover the top and sides.

2 Cut apart the rose picks to make six single roses with 1" stems. Glue the roses evenly spaced around the wreath. Cut the nigella into 2"–2½" sprigs and glue clusters of three between the roses.

3 Cut the larkspur into 3" sprigs and glue evenly spaced among the caspia. Cut the hill flowers into 3"–3½" sprigs and wire together in clusters of five. Glue evenly spaced throughout the floral materials.

4 Cut the brisa media and plumosus into 3" sprigs and glue in clusters of two or three evenly spaced around the wreath. Use the ribbon to make an oblong bow (see page 26) with a center loop, six 2" loops, two 3" loops and one 18" tail. Glue the bow to the inside handle bottom and wrap the tail spiral fashion around the handle to the opposite side; glue to secure.

As we decorate our homes for Christmas, one of the first tasks is to hang the wreath on the front door to welcome family and friends throughout the holidays. Choices of colors and styles are numerous when using silk and dried materials to make wreaths. And when stored carefully, wreaths can be enjoyed for many Christmases to come.

Within the following pages we've put together a great collection featuring various styles and color combinations using a vast array of materials. Some products are unusual, while many others are natural choices for Christmas decorating. Poinsettias, holly, pine cones, angels, reindeer, berries and red roses all are standard materials for Christmas decorations. To spice things up, we've added red poppies, tapestry ribbon, rice grass, paper ribbon fans, dried pomegranates, peach roses and protea flats (dried flowers which look like pine cone sections).

We're very pleased with the results! All the designs are wonderful additions and accents for your home, adding a cozy Christmas feeling wherever they are placed.

Whether you decorate with red and green, gold and ivory, burgundy and hunter green or in naturals for Christmas, we've presented a wealth of possibilities for gorgeous decorations to bring the warmth of the season into your home.

The Christmas Magnolias design on page 117 features the wonderful color combination of ivory and gold. The gold mesh ribbon and berries look great when mixed with ivory magnolias and preserved fir branches. More gold touches are found in the Wreath with Berries on page 125 and the Poinsettia & Pine Wreath on page 119. In both of these designs the gold is an accent to the stronger reds and greens.

Gold has a much stronger presence in the Rose & Pine Crescent Wreath on page 122. It is the dominant color with burgundy and greens as accent colors. Gold, when mixed with other colors, adds shine and sparkle to a wreath, whether used profusely or just in light touches.

A section on Christmas wreaths wouldn't be complete without some reference to music and we've provided that with the Musical Instrument Wreath on page 118. Gold instruments and musical notes have been attached among the pine, then, echoing that theme, a red ribbon featuring musical notes is looped and tucked throughout the design.

We haven't left out the naturals, either. The Woodland Wreath on page 124 is filled with latex fruit, twigs and dried materials, all nestled among the mixed evergreens of the wreath base. The tapestry ribbon may seem a little formal, but it looks terrific with all those dark colors.

More natural products can be found throughout the section, including rattan bells, carved wooden ornaments which have been stained, as well as numerous dried materials such as German statice, rice grass, pine cones and realistic berries.

To carry one theme throughout the house, simply use the same or similar products to create matching centerpieces, garlands, swags and tree decorations. Special touches to the tree can be as simple as tying sprigs of floral materials together with a ribbon and nestling the cluster down among the tree branches.

This section is filled with an abundance of ideas and options to help you make your home cozy, or elegant, or nostalgic for Christmas—whichever is your preference. We've provided techniques and designs for spectacular wreaths to be hung and placed throughout your home, bringing the warmth of the season into every room!

Angel Wreath

14"x17" TWIGS™ oval wreath with
  vine lattice back
10" long TWIGS™ teardrop wreath
10½" tall abaca angel
2 stems of green vinyl Canadian pine,
  each with 3 branches of seven 5" sprigs
2 stems of artificial burgundy
  blackberries, each with seven 1½" long berries
1 stem of cream latex dogwood with five 3" wide blossoms
  and leaves
2 poinsettia/pine picks, each with a 6" burgundy blossom and
  five 4"–5" leaves, three ¾"–1½" fruits, three 5" pine sprigs
  and a 1½" cone
½ oz. of natural dried rice grass
2½ yards of 2⅝" wide burgundy/dark green/bronze tapestry ribbon
15" of white/gold ¼" wide round braid
24" of natural jute, 12" of ½" wide gold braid
24" of ½" wide natural cotton braid
24-gauge wire, low temperature glue gun and sticks

1 Cut 4" of round braid; glue the ends to the back of the angel's head for a halo. Tie the jute around her waist in a shoestring bow (see page 24) with 1" loops, a 5" and a 7" tail; knot the ends. Glue two 11" lengths of natural braid around the bottom of her dress, one just above the other. Glue the gold braid over their center and round braid around the bottom edge.

2 Attach a wire hanger (see page 18) to the top back of the oval wreath. Cut the binding vines off the teardrop wreath; reshape the wreath into four loops. Insert the ends into the bottom of the oval wreath so the loops extend forward in a fan, forming a shelf. Cut the branches off a pine stem. Glue one on each side, extending upward 15" from the center bottom. Glue the third at the center bottom, extending over the shelf. Glue the angel onto the pine.

3 Cut a berry stem into two 7" sprigs. Glue one on each side among the pine branches. Cut each poinsettia pick to 7" and glue one on each side. Cut the dogwood into a 1-blossom and two 2-blossom sprigs, each 7"–8" long. Shape the petals, then glue a 2-blossom sprig on each side among the berries and the 1-blossom sprig to the shelf center, extending forward.

4 Use the wide ribbon to make a puffy bow (see page 26) with a center loop, six 4¼" loops and 12"–14" tails. Glue under the shelf. Cut the remaining berry stem into a 1-berry and two 3-berry sprigs; glue a 3-berry sprig extending forward and one right of the bow. Glue the 1-berry sprig on the left. Cut two 7" branches off the last pine stem; glue one on each side of the bow. Cut the sprigs off the remaining branch and glue to fill empty spaces along the sides and front of the wreath. Cut 6"–10" rice grass sprigs and glue evenly spaced through the arrangement.

bottom view

Christmas Magnolias

22" TWIGS™
open-weave vine
wreath
3 yards of 2¾" wide
gold open-weave
wire mesh ribbon
1⅔ yards of 4" wide
ivory/gold
tapestry ribbon
with wired edges
2 branches of silk
magnolias, each
with one 7", one
5" and one 4"
blossom, a bud
and many leaves
8 oz. of green pre-
served Frazier fir
2 oz. of dried caspia
6 artificial gold berry
picks, each with
twelve ⅜" wide
berries
white spray paint
24-gauge wire
low temperature glue
gun and sticks

1 Lightly spray paint the wreath for a white-washed look. Wrap 1⅓ yards of mesh ribbon spiral fashion over ⅓ of the right wreath, leaving 1" between wraps; glue in place. Shape the magnolias and bend each branch to follow the curve of the wreath. Lay the stems end to end on the left side with 7" between the large blossoms; wire securely.

2 Cut the fir into 6"–9" sprigs. Set aside 10–12 shorter sprigs; glue the remaining sprigs evenly spaced among the magnolias. Use the tapestry ribbon to make a puffy bow (see page 26) with two 5" loops, an 18" and a 12" tail. Glue the bow over the magnolia stems; tuck the 18" tail below the lower magnolias and weave the 12" tail among the upper ones as shown. Use the remaining mesh ribbon to make a puffy bow with a center loop, two 4" loops and 24" tails. Glue to the center of the tapestry bow; knot the tail ends and weave among the magnolias and fir. Glue the remaining fir sprigs around the bow loops.

3 Cut the caspia into 6"–9" sprigs. Glue them evenly spaced among the materials.

4 Glue one berry pick above and one below the lower large magnolia; glue a pick between the large blossom and the end of each branch as shown in the large photo. Divide each of the last two berry picks in half. Glue a small cluster near the tip of each magnolia branch, then glue one above and one below the upper large magnolia.

Musical Instrument Wreath

28" vinyl wreath of assorted evergreens with pine
    cones
5⅓ yards of 2" wide red/green/gold holiday musical
    note ribbon with wired edges
one 5" long gold trumpet
one 5" long gold French horn
two 4" long gold musical notes
two 2½" gold jingle bells
3 stems of red/burgundy berries, each with seven
    1¼"wide berries
ten 2" wide red silk rose picks
1 oz. of dried German statice
gold glitter spray
24-gauge wire
low temperature glue gun and sticks

1 Fluff the wreath branches. Cut 2⅓ yards of ribbon. Glue the ends into the wreath top; tuck and glue the rest of the length in five places equally spaced around the wreath. Use the remaining ribbon to make a puffy bow (see page 26) with a center loop, ten 3½" loops and 14" tails. Glue over the ribbon ends.

2 Twist one end of a 6" wire length through the hanger of a bell, then twist the other end into the wreath so the bell hangs below the bow. Wire and glue the remaining bell, instruments and notes over the glued areas of the ribbon. Cut two berry stems to 10" long; glue one on each side of the bow. Cut the remaining berry sprig stems to 4" and glue one below each musical note and instrument.

3 Cut the rose stems to 2". Glue one rose on each side of each note, each instrument and the lower bell.

4 Cut the statice into 4"–6" sprigs and glue evenly spaced throughout the wreath and among the bow loops. Spray the entire wreath with glitter.

Poinsettia & Spruce Wreath

24"x 2" TWIGS™ stick wreath
5 yards of 2½"wide green/red poinsettia print wire-edged ribbon
5 yards of ⅜" wide gold mesh wired ribbon
5 green vinyl pine picks, each with twelve 5" sprigs
1 silk poinsettia and holly bush with 8 branches of poinsettias, each with a 6" wide blossom, and 6 branches of holly, each with 3" long leaves and red berries
1 oz. of preserved baby's breath
gold spray paint

1 Cut 2½ yards of poinsettia ribbon and wrap the wreath spiral fashion with wraps 4"–6" apart; glue the ends at the lower front, leaving a 9" gap. Cut 3½ yards of gold ribbon. Starting at the same point as the first ribbon, loosely weave it back and forth over the front of the wreath, gluing to secure. Wire one pine stem to the bottom right over the ribbon ends. Wire another above the first, tucking the base behind the tip of the first stem. Repeat on the left as shown.

2 Use the remaining poinsettia ribbon to make a puffy bow (see page 26) with a center loop, six 4½" loops, an 8" and a 10" tail. Use the remaining gold ribbon to make a puffy bow with no center loop and eight 3" loops. Insert the gold bow under the center loop of the first bow and fan the loops as shown.

3 Cut the poinsettia and holly branches to 3". Glue a poinsettia on each side of the bow and one above it. On each side, glue a poinsettia near the tip of the pine and another halfway between the bow and the tip. Glue the last to the wreath center top. Glue two holly sprigs next to each poinsettia on each side of the bow and one tucked into the bow bottom as shown. Cut the leaves off the remaining holly sprig and glue them evenly spaced around the top poinsettia. Cut the sprigs off the remaining pine stem and glue around the upper poinsettia among the holly leaves.

4 Spray the baby's breath gold; cut it into 2"–3" sprigs and glue evenly spaced among the poinsettias, holly sprigs and bow loops.

Heart Wreath

two 36" stems of latex silk cherries, each with
*   nine ¾"–1" wide cherries and many leaves*
one 5' long dusty green silk holly garland
2 latex apple/berry picks, each with a 2¾" long
*   quarter apple, five ½" wide red/orange*
*   berries, two 1"–1¼" wide green fruits, and 6*
*   leaves*
2 latex apple/pine Christmas picks, each with a
*   1½" wide apple, a 2" long pine cone, 6*
*   selignum pods, three ⅝" wide green/bur-*
*   gundy berries, 3 pine sprigs and holly leaves*
2 clusters of green/burgundy artificial grapes,
*   each with 2 sprigs of seven ½"–¾"grapes*
*   and leaves*
1 oz. of dried German statice
4½ yards of 1⅜" wide red velvet ribbon with
*   gold wired edges*
24-gauge wire
low temperature glue gun and sticks

1 Wire the ends of the cherry stems together, then curve the upper portions down as shown, forming a heart. Wire the tips together at the bottom. Attach a wire loop hanger (see page 18) to each side of the upper back.

2 Wire one end of the garland to the center top. Wrap it spiral fashion to completely cover the wreath; wire to secure the other end.

3 Beginning at the center of one side, wire an apple/berry pick to extend up along the heart shoulder, an apple/pine pick to extend down and a grape cluster below that, extending nearly to the bottom point. Repeat for the other side.

4 Cut 2 yards of ribbon. Beginning at the center top, tuck and glue it throughout the front. Use the remaining ribbon to make an oblong bow (see page 26) with a center loop, ten 1½"–2" loops and 12" tails. Glue over the ribbon ends. Cut the statice into 4"–7" sprigs. Glue them evenly spaced around the wreath following the lines of the nearby materials, as shown in the large photo.

St. Nicholas Wreath

22" wide honeysuckle wreath
9' long green vinyl fir garland
12" tall fabric woodland St.
 Nicholas tree topper holding an
 evergreen garland with berries
 and cones
3 yards of 2⅝"wide of burgundy/
 green/gold floral print ribbon
 with gold wired edges
4 yards of ⅞" wide gold wired
 mesh ribbon
8 strands of 48" long raffia
1 oz. of purple preserved statice
 sinuata
1 oz. of gold glittered dried
 German statice
2 stems of burgundy berries, each
 with six sprigs of five ⅜" wide
 berries
16 dried red roses with 2" stems
gold glitter spray
24-gauge wire
low temperature glue gun and
 sticks

3 Cut the gold statice into 3"–5" sprigs. Hold 4–5 sprigs together and glue to the center front of a garland wrap. Repeat around the wreath. Glue the remaining sprigs evenly spaced throughout the garland front. Cut the purple statice into 3"–5" sprigs. Make clusters of three sprigs and glue one into the center of each gold statice cluster. Glue the remaining sprigs as for the gold sprigs.

4 Cut the berry sprigs to 3"–4". Glue two sprigs angled outward from each statice circle as shown. Cut the berries off one sprig; glue three into St. Nicholas' garland and two into his hat. Glue one rose into his garland and three into the center of each statice cluster. Spray the entire design with gold glitter.

1 Fluff the garland, then wire one end to the wreath back. Wrap it spiral fashion around the wreath, keeping the wraps 8"–9" apart.

2 Glue one end of the print ribbon to the back of the wreath and wrap it spiral fashion between the garland wraps; glue the end to the beginning. Shred the raffia into fine ¹⁄₁₆"–⅛" wide strands and weave evenly throughout the garland. Wrap the gold ribbon over the garland center. Glue two 24-gauge wires to the inside of the St. Nicholas. Wire him to the inside bottom of the wreath over the garland.

Rose & Pine Crescent Wreath

1 Glue one end of the ribbon to the wreath bottom and wrap spiral fashion, with the wraps 4"–5" apart. Glue the end over the beginning and cut off the excess ribbon. Remove four 5"–6" long sprigs from the bottom of each pine branch and set aside for step 4. Cut the branches to 13". Place them end to end at the bottom front, leaving a 4" space between the bottom sprigs on each stem. Wire each stem in two or three places to secure.

2 Knot 2" from each end of the cord; unravel the ends. Glue one end of the cord in the open area, leaving a 9" tail; wrap it spiral fashion between the ribbon wraps. Glue the end, leaving a 12" tail. Use the ribbon to make a puffy bow (see page 26) with a center loop, eight 4" loops, a 12" and 16" tail. Wire to the open area at the bottom.

3 Cut the pick stems to 2". Glue one above the bow and one in the bow center. Glue one on each side of the bow among the pine sprigs. Spray gold paint onto the plastic wrap, making a puddle. Gently dip the tip of each rose petal and bud in the paint, gilding the edges. Cut the roses to 5" long and glue a rose on each side of the bow.

4 Glue the remaining pine sprigs evenly spaced among the upper bow loops. Cut the statice into 2"–3" sprigs and glue evenly spaced throughout the pine sprigs and bow loops.

18" wide lacquered grapevine wreath
5½ yards of 2⅝" wide sheer metallic gold wire-edged ribbon
3 yards of ⅜" wide metallic gold cord
2 branches of green vinyl pine, each with twenty-one 5"–6" long sprigs
2 stems of burgundy silk roses, each with five 2" wide blooms and 2 buds

4 metallic gold Christmas picks, each with a 2" long gold pine cone, 1" package, 1½" wide apple and foliage
1 oz. of gold glittered dried German statice
gold spray paint, plastic wrap
24-gauge wire
low temperature glue gun and sticks

Gold Fan Wreath

18" wide honeysuckle wreath

2 stems of green vinyl pine, each with 3 branches of eight 5" long sprigs

3⅓ yards of 2½" wide paper lace ribbon

4 yards of 1½" wide metallic gold/ivory wire-edged ribbon

3 yards of ⅜" wide metallic gold braid

4 Christmas picks, each with one 1½" wide gold apple, one 2" long gold-tipped pine cone, one 1" gold-wrapped package and sprigs of fir, holly and gold foliage

1 stem of white silk Queen Anne's lace with twelve 1½"–2" wide blossom clusters

gold spray paint

gold glitter spray

24-gauge wire, stapler, staples

low temperature glue gun and sticks

1 Cut the paper ribbon into ten 12" lengths. Place two lengths side by side, overlapping ½", and glue together. Accordion-fold into a fan and staple at the bottom. Repeat with the remaining ribbon lengths. Spray paint each side of each fan gold; let dry.

2 Cut each pine stem into three 12" branches. Cut a 5" lower sprig off each branch and set aside for step 3. Arrange three branches to extend from 11:00 over the wreath top to 2:00; wire to secure. Repeat from 11:00 down to 6:00, leaving an 8" open area at the lower right.

3 Use the ribbon to make a puffy bow (see page 26) with twelve 3½" loops and 26" tails. Glue to the wreath at the upper left between the pine stems. Use the braid to make a loopy bow (see page 27) with a center loop, ten 2½" loops and 28" tails. Glue the braid bow to the center of the ribbon bow. Glue the pine sprigs from step 1 around the bow.

4 Cut the stem of each Christmas pick to 2"; glue one on each side of the bow and another 6" away on each side. Glue a fan behind the bow and one near each pick as shown in the large photo. Cut the Queen Anne's lace blossom clusters off the main stem and trim each to 1½" long. Glue them evenly spaced among all the materials. Spray the wreath with gold glitter. Attach a wire hanger (see page 18) to the top back.

Woodland Wreath

26" wide vinyl mixed evergreen wreath with assorted cones

4 wired stems of natural grapevine twigs, each with 3 sprigs of three 9" long twigs

2 latex apple branches, each with one 1½" and three 1" wide red apples and many leaves

2 stems of burgundy artificial berries, each with 7 sprigs of five ⅜" wide berries

4 yards of 2⅝" wide burgundy/brown/gold tapestry wire-edged ribbon

3 oz. of preserved brown eucalyptus

7 dried protea flats ————————

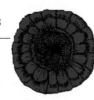

2 oz. of dried canella

24-gauge wire

low temperature glue gun and sticks

1 Cut the apple branches to 24". Wire them to the wreath top extending down each side and leaving a 9" gap. Cut each grapevine stem into three 9" sprigs. Glue six twigs on each side, evenly spaced among the apple sprigs.

2 Use 2⅓ yards of ribbon to make an oblong bow (see page 26) with a center loop, ten 2½"–3½" loops and 10" tails. Wire to the wreath top. Cut the eucalyptus into 7"–12" sprigs. Glue them evenly spaced throughout the apple and twig sprigs and around the bow loops, gluing shorter sprigs near the bow and longer ones near the branch ends.

3 Cut the protea stems to 3". Glue one under the bow and three evenly spaced down each side as shown.

4 Fold the remaining ribbon, making a 18" and a 20" tail. Glue the fold under the bow so the tails extend down. Cut each berry stem into seven 4" sprigs. Glue one sprig in the bow center, two sprigs on each side above the bow, and the rest evenly spaced among the protea blossoms and apples. Cut the canella into 2"–4" sprigs. Glue them spaced evenly among the bow loops, berries and apple branches.

Berries & Pine Wreath

18" wide root wreath
2½ yards of 3" wide gold-brushed dark green paper ribbon
3¾ yards of ½" wide gold twisted cord
5 stems of green vinyl pine, each with three 7" sprigs
5 red artificial blackberry picks, each with three 1"–1¼" berries and 3 leaves
2 oz. of natural dried bupleurum
1 oz. of natural dried rice grass
24-gauge wire
low temperature glue gun and sticks

1 Glue one pine stem into the wreath at the lower right, extending downward. Cut the sprigs off the remaining pine stems. Glue three into the roots just above the first stem, angled to cover the stem end. Glue the rest evenly spaced into the wreath, angled as shown, leaving ¼ of the wreath bare at the lower left.

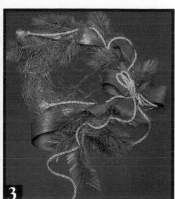

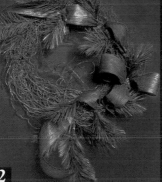

2 Cut a 64" length of paper ribbon. Loop and glue it among the pine sprigs as shown with a 14" tail extending behind the bottom stem. Use the remaining ribbon to make a collar bow (see page 24) with two 4½" loops; glue it at the right center of the wreath.

3 Cut an 82" cord length; knot and fray the ends. Loop and glue the cord among the pine sprigs and ribbon. Use the remaining cord to make a loopy bow with four 3" loops and 12" tails. Glue it over the ribbon bow.

4 Glue a berry pick to extend over the bottom pine stem. Glue another pick below the bows and three evenly spaced above the bows. Cut the bupleurum and rice grass into 6"–8" sprigs. Glue them evenly spaced among the pine and berries, angling them in similar directions. Attach a wire loop hanger (see page 18) to the top back of the wreath.

Reindeer Centerpiece

10" tall plush jointed reindeer
½ yard of ¼" wide metallic red braided cord
2½ yards of 1⅜" wide red/green plaid ribbon
5 silk holly picks, each with many ⅜" round
  red berries and three 1" long acorns, holly
  leaves and pine sprigs
9' long green vinyl garland of assorted ever-
  greens with natural pine cones
1 oz. of red dried canella
½ oz. of dried German statice
24-gauge wire
low temperature glue gun and sticks

1 Fluff the garland sprigs. Fold the garland in half and twist the halves together, forming a 4½' garland. Form the center of this length into a 10" wide circle with two 13" ends; wire the lengths where they cross. Position the ends to angle off the wreath in opposite directions.

2 Tie the red cord around the reindeer's neck, knotting under his chin. Unravel the cord ends. Wire the reindeer to the left front wreath bottom. Use the ribbon to make an oblong bow (see page 26) with a center loop, ten 1½"–3" long loops and 15" tails. Glue to the inside wreath bottom, just right of the reindeer.

3 Cut the holly picks to 4". Glue one in front of the bow, one to the wreath top above the bow and one in the middle of the right side opposite the reindeer. Glue a pick one in the center of each extending end as shown.

4 Cut the statice and canella into 2"–4" sprigs. Glue them evenly spaced among the evergreen sprigs on the centerpiece front and back.

126 – Christmas Wreaths

Square Wreath

16"x1" TWIGS™ square wreath
three 3½" tall rattan bells
3' vinyl evergreen garland
2 stems of red silk poppies, each with
   a 5" wide poppy, an open bud and
   a closed bud
1 yard of ¼" wide metallic red
   braided cord
2 yards of 2⅜" wide brown paper
   musical note wire-edged ribbon
6 silk raspberry picks, each with
   seven ⅝" wide red, green and burgundy berries and leaves
1 oz. of green preserved ming fern
24-gauge wire
low temperature glue gun and sticks

1 Wire the garland around the inside of the square. Cut the cord into one 15", one 12" and one 9" length. Tie a bell to the end of each length, leaving a 1" tail. Wire the other cord ends together in the wreath center top.

2 Use the ribbon to make an oblong bow (see page 26) with a center loop, eight 1"–3½" loops, a 7" and a 9" tail. Glue at the top center of the wreath as shown.

3 Cut a poppy with a 4" stem; glue it below left of the bow. Cut the other poppy with a 2" stem; glue it just right of the bow. Cut each bud with a 4" stem. Glue a closed bud to extend from under each poppy; glue an open bud extending left from the bow and one just left of the left bell. Cut the leaves off the stems and glue one near each poppy and bud.

4 Glue five berry picks evenly spaced around the square. Cut the last pick into a 3-berry and a 4-berry sprig; glue one above and one below the bow as shown in the large photo. Turn the wreath over and cut 6–8 long fine twigs from the back (choose ones that won't show from the front). Cut the fern into 7"–8" sprigs. Glue the fern and twigs evenly spaced among the pine sprigs and bow loops. Make a wire hanger (see page 18) at the top back.

Evergreen & Ivy Wreath

30" wide green vinyl sugar pine wreath
three 5" tall carved wooden ornaments:
   1 Santa, 1 rocking horse, 1 tree
3 yards of 2¾" wide green/rust/gold
   tapestry ribbon
2 apple/cone picks, each with a 1½" wide
   green apple, a 1½" long cone, three ¾"
   wide green berries, 2 clusters of ¼"
   wide peach berries, 3 pine sprigs and 6
   holly leaves
3 gold-brushed rose/cone picks, each with
   a 3" and a 1½" wide peach rose, a 2"
   long rust cone, a 1" long green cone, 5
   grape leaves, many berries and pods
1 stem of green silk English ivy with 14
   sprigs of five 1½"–2" wide leaves
walnut acrylic wood stain
1" wide paintbrush, clean cloth
spray wood sealer
24-gauge wire
low temperature glue gun and sticks

1 Seal the ornaments. Apply stain, wipe off and let dry. Fluff the wreath sprigs. Use the ribbon to make a puffy bow (see page 26) with a 3" center loop, six 4" loops, a 15" and a 30" tail. Glue the bow and ornaments equally spaced around the wreath, with the bow at the upper left.

2 Cut the rose picks apart. Glue a large rose, two rust cones and two leaves between the bow and tree. Glue a large rose, a rust cone, a green cone and two leaves between the horse and Santa. Glue a large and a small rose, a green cone and two leaves between the bow and Santa; glue two small roses, a green cone and two leaves between the horse and tree. Glue the remaining leaves, pods and berries evenly spaced around the wreath.

3 Cut the apple picks apart. Glue an apple right of the tree and one right of Santa. Glue a peach berry cluster below the horse and two below the upper apple. Glue a green berry cluster above the horse's tail and one above the bow. Glue the remaining components evenly spaced around the wreath.

4 Cut the ivy sprigs off the stem and glue evenly spaced around the wreath, tucking them among the pine sprigs. Loop the 15" ribbon tail up and glue above the bow. Loop and glue the 30" tail down the left side. Attach a wire loop hanger (see page 18) to the top back.

Baby's First Christmas

18" wide vinyl evergreen wreath with mixed pine cones
12" plush teddy bear with jointed arms and legs
2⅓ yards of 1⅜" wide peach sheer wire-edged ribbon
6 stems of peach parchment miniature roses, each with a 1½" wide blossom
1 oz. of white dried starflowers
1 oz. of dried rice grass
four 1½" wooden blocks
24 assorted ¾" tall wooden letters and numbers
peach acrylic paint, paintbrush
24-gauge wire
low temperature glue gun and sticks

1 Remove the cones from a 10" section on the left side of the wreath and set aside for step 3. Wrap 9" of ribbon around the bear's neck; glue the ends under her chin. Wrap a wire around the bear's neck and one around her left leg; wire her to the left wreath where the cones were removed. Use 9" of ribbon to make a collar bow (see page 24) with 2" loops and 2" tails; glue under her chin.

2 Glue one end of the remaining ribbon under the bear's leg. Loop and tuck the ribbon around the wreath front, gluing it into the pine sprigs every 3"–4". Drape the end over the bear's left paw, leaving a 5" tail, and glue. Cut the rose stems to 1". Glue one rose to the ribbon on the paw and one to each glued area as shown.

3 Hold 6–12 starflowers together at varying heights and cut the stems 1" below the lowest flower; glue the cluster among the pine sprigs. Repeat for a total of 14–16 clusters; glue evenly spaced throughout the wreath. Glue the cones from step 1 to the pine sprigs on the bear's right side and to fill any other open areas.

4 Cut the rice grass into 4"–8" sprigs. Glue them evenly spaced throughout the wreath. Paint the blocks. Glue a letter or a number to the center of each face. Glue one block to the bear's right leg and the others evenly spaced around the wreath as shown in the large photo.

Fresh Evergreen Wreath

16" wide wire wreath ring
8–10 lbs. of assorted fresh evergreen branches: Douglas fir, noble fir, cedar
3 stems of burgundy leaf poinsettias, each with a 10" blossom and 2 leaves
   (or use silk poinsettias)
2 stems of burgundy acrylic grapes, each with 2 clusters of many ½"–¾"
   wide burgundy/red grapes and many sage green frosted leaves
3½ yards of 2⅝" wide burgundy/sage green tapestry wire-edged ribbon
1 oz. of light green preserved plumosus
22-gauge paddle wire
low temperature glue gun and sticks

2 Wire the grape branches to the wreath front as shown, leaving open space at the upper left and lower right.

3 Use the ribbon to make an oblong bow (see page 26) with a center loop, ten 3"–4" loops, a 24" and a 30" tail. Wire the bow into the upper left open area; weave the 24" tail down the right side and the 30" tail down the left side. Cut the poinsettia stems to 4". Glue one poinsettia on each side of the bow and one between the grape clusters on the left side as shown in the photo. Cut the leaf sprigs off the stem and glue around the poinsettias.

1 Cut the greenery into 7"–10" sprigs. Cluster 8–10 assorted sprigs together. Attach the end of the paddle wire to the wreath frame; wire the cluster in place, securely wrapping 3–4 times around the bottom 2" of the stems. Repeat around the wreath, wiring each cluster so the top conceals the stems of the previous cluster.

4 Cut the plumosus into 5"–9" sprigs. Glue the shorter sprigs around the bow and among the bow loops. Glue the longer sprigs evenly spaced among the grapes and poinsettias. Attach a wire loop hanger (see page 18) to the top back.

Reva's Pod & Cone Wreath

20" round Styrofoam® wreath
6 oz. of gray excelsior
100–110 assorted 1½"–3" wide pine
   and spruce cones
three 3" wide dried pomegranates
two 3" wide dried lotus pods
two 3" long dried fiber pods on picks
two 1¾" wide dried mehogni pods on
   picks
clear gloss acrylic spray
monofilament nylon fishing line
wire cutters
22-gauge wire (for cones)
20" of 16-gauge wire (for hanger)
low temperature glue gun and sticks

1 Cover the wreath with excelsior, wrapping spiral fashion with the nylon line to secure it. Wrap one end of the 16-gauge wire around the wreath top, form a 2" loop at the top back, then wrap the rest of the wire around the wreath.

2 Trim one side of a cone to fit against the inside of the wreath. Cut a 6" wire length and wrap it around the cone center; twist close to the cone to secure, leaving the ends extending on the cut side. Dip the wire ends in glue and insert into the wreath. Repeat to cover the inside of the wreath with cones, then to cover the outside.

3 Trim, wire and attach additional cones to sparsely cover the wreath front, varying the angles and leaving open areas among the cones.

4 Glue a lotus pod at the center top and another at the bottom. Glue a pomegranate near the lower lotus pod and the others pomegranates evenly spaced around the wreath. Glue a hairy pod to each side of the outer wreath, one at 7:30 and one at 3:30. Glue the mehogni pods to the inside of the wreath opposite the hairy pods. Fill in the remaining empty spaces with cones, turning some bottom up and some point up, trimming them as needed to fit. Spray the entire wreath with gloss acrylic; let dry; repeat.

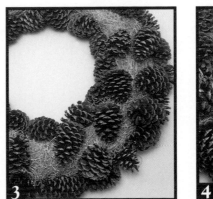

Not Your Average, Ordinary Wreath

*W*hen one thinks of wreaths, a round shape comes to mind, usually decorated with materials and hanging on a wall. Well, in this section, we've taken ordinary round wreaths one step further. We've included unusual shapes as bases and added subtle twists to the designs, making each of them an unusual addition to home decorating.

In the Rattan & Doily Wreath on page 136, an ordinary rattan wreath is turned into a sweet, romantic piece simply by adding a doily to the center. For a more natural look, the Wreath In A Wreath on page 137 combines raffia with a vine wreath, adding delicacy without sacrificing the natural feeling. And, speaking of raffia, the Raffia Wreath on page 142 is made completely from that leaf material. Pods, feathers, fruit slices and silk flowers are added to enhance the curves yet maintain the wildness of the piece.

Creative uses have been made of ordinary wreath bases in this section, or unusual wreath forms have been used to construct the projects. If you have need of a distinctive wreath design, check out the projects within these pages, then have fun exploring the possibilities available using wreaths in creative ways.

Bird in a Twig Loop

TWIGS™ crossed oval vine wreaths: one 9"x12", one 12"x18"
2¼ yards of 1⅜" wide tan/rust/peach tapestry ribbon
3½" long orange/brown mushroom bird
1 branch of maroon latex plums with four 1"–1¾" wide plums
   and many 2" long leaves
2 stems of variegated latex maroon/orange maple leaves, each
   with five 3"–4" wide leaves, 2 orange/maroon mini berry
   clusters and grass sprigs
2 stems of rust silk mini carnations, each with four 1½" wide
   blossoms
2 stems of orange/red silk honeysuckle, each with three 8"–10"
   long sprigs of 3 blossom clusters
twelve 2" long dried red chili peppers
24-gauge wire
low temperature glue gun and sticks

1 Cut off and save the twig ends from the small wreath, making it teardrop-shaped. Wire it inside the large wreath as shown. Glue the reserved twig ends evenly spaced among the twig ends on the large wreath for a fuller appearance. Bend the plum branch to curve over the top of the large wreath; wire in 2–3 spots to secure and trim the excess stem.

2 Cut the maple leaf stems to 12". Wire one over the plum branch. Wire the other at the tip of the first to extend around the left side of the loop.

3 Use the ribbon to make a puffy bow (see page 26) with a center loop, six 3½" loops, an 11" and a 17" tail. Glue over the wired area of the twig loops. Glue the 17" tail to the lower wreath front as shown. Glue the bird to the inner wreath center. Cut each carnation blossom with a 2" stem. Glue evenly spaced among the plum sprigs and around the bow loops as shown in the large photo.

4 Cut the honeysuckle into 3" blossom sprigs. Glue two above and two below the bow and the rest evenly spaced among the floral materials. Glue the peppers near the honeysuckle stems. Make a wire loop hanger (see page 18) at the top back.

4"x4½" terra cotta pot

6"x5" split bamboo basket with no handle

1 green silk ivy bush with six 10", five 8" and
   six 6" branches of 1½"–2" wide leaves

3 stems of artificial burgundy raspberries, each
   with two clusters of five ⅝" wide berries and
   many 1¼" wide leaves

six 1" wide artificial red apples

six 1" wide artificial yellow pears

12 stems of peach parchment roses, each with
   one 1½" rose

½ oz. of green American Moss™ excelsior

1 oz. of preserved baby's breath

2⅔ yards of 1½" wide sheer lavender/green floral print ribbon

wire clothes hanger, wire cutters

plaster of Paris, bowl, large spoon, water

24-gauge wire

low temperature glue gun and sticks

1 Bend the clothes hanger into a circle,
straighten the hook and trim to 4". Mix
the plaster and pour into the flower pot;
insert the straightened hook into the plaster,
centering the circle. Allow to harden. Place
the flower pot in the basket.

2 Cover the top of the plaster with excelsior. Cut the branches off the ivy bush.
Set aside two 6" branches for step 4. Starting
at the bottom center, wrap 10" branches spiral fashion around the wire wreath. Wrap the
shorter branches over the longer branches,
filling the wreath evenly; wire to secure.

3 Cut the raspberry stems into 5" sprigs;
glue them evenly spaced among the ivy
leaves on the front and back of the wreath.
Repeat with the apples and pears. Cut the
rose stems to 3" and glue evenly spaced to
both sides.

4 Cut the baby's breath into 2"–3" sprigs
and glue evenly spaced among the ivy
leaves and around the base. Glue a 6" ivy
branch on each side of the base. Use the
ribbon to make a puffy bow (see page 26)
with a center loop, four 3" loops and 7" tails.
Glue the bow into the wreath at the center
bottom with a tail extending down each side
of the basket. Loosely tuck and glue the
remaining ribbon around the wreath as
shown in the large photo.

Rattan & Doily Wreath

8" round rattan wreath
8" round white lace doily
1½ yards of 1⅜"wide white lace/mauve satin ribbon
2 stems of mauve silk mini roses, each with 2 sprigs
 of four ¾" blossoms
1 stem of white silk star of Bethlehem with many
 1"–1½" blossoms and small buds
1 oz. of pink dried ti tree
½ oz. of preserved green myrii foliage
white spray paint
24-gauge wire
low temperature glue gun and sticks

1 Spray the wreath white; let dry. Wire the doily to the wreath back in four places; glue to secure.

2 Cut the myrii into two 8", two 5" and two 3" sprigs. Glue an 8" sprig to the left center of the wreath, extending upward. Glue a 5" sprig to the right of it and a 3" sprig to the left. Glue an 8" sprig extending downward and slightly right with a 5" sprig to the left and a 3" sprig to the right of it. Cut the ti tree into 3"–9" sprigs. Set half aside for step 3. Glue a 9" sprig extending to the upper right and one extending to the lower right. Glue the rest evenly spaced as shown.

3 Use the ribbon to make a puffy bow (see page 26) with a center loop, eight 2½" loops and 5" tails. Wire it between the upper and lower design areas. Cut the rose stems as follows: two 7" long 2-rose sprigs, two 4" long 2-rose sprigs, the rest into 1"–2" long 1-rose sprigs. Glue the 7" sprigs in front of the 8" myrii sprigs and the 4" sprigs in front of the 5" myrii sprigs. Glue the remaining roses around the bow. Glue the remaining ti tree sprigs evenly spaced among the roses and bow loops.

4 Cut the star of Bethlehem blossoms and buds into 2"–4" sprigs. Glue larger blossoms near the bow and smaller blossoms and buds toward the ends of the design areas, evenly spaced among the flowers and bow loops. Make a wire loop hanger (see page 18) at the top back.

Raffia Wreath

5 oz. of coarse raffia (or use abaca fiber)
2 stems of coral silk poppies, each with three 4" wide blossoms and 4 buds
3 stems of silk hazelnuts, each with three 6"–11" sprigs of 1" wide nuts
2 stems of yellow parchment forsythia, each with three 9"–16" sprigs of 1" long blossoms
pheasant feathers: two 18", five 6"–8" long
four 4"–7" long dried chili peppers
3 dried orange slices
5 dried okra pod picks
1 fiber ball pod
2 eskira pods
30-gauge wire
low temperature glue gun and sticks

1 Coil the raffia into a 15" wreath with the upper stems curling to the inside and 40" tails extending downward; wire. Place a hazelnut stem over the wired area to extend 19" down to the right. Place another over it to extend 14". Place the third extending 18" over the top of the wreath to the left. Wire to secure the stems.

2 Place a forsythia stem over the left hazelnut stem and one over the right one; wire. Trim any excess forsythia stem ends. Cut the poppy stems to 15"; wire them end to end over the forsythia. Glue three okra pods among the right flowers and two among the left ones.

3 Glue one pepper angled upward and three angled downward over the wired area. Glue an eskira pod angled upward, then glue another and the fiber ball pod angled downward. Glue a long feather and three short ones evenly spaced among the right flowers. Glue the other long feather and two short ones evenly spaced among the left flowers.

4 Glue the smallest orange slice above the fiber ball pod. Tear the others in half and glue the pieces among the pods, angled outward. Cut three nuts from hidden areas; glue them among the pods and fruit. Attach a wire hanger (see page 18) to the upper back.

Potted Garden in a Wreath

15" round grapevine wreath
4" tall terra cotta flower pot
1 stem of white silk spirea with a 20" section of 15 sprigs of
    a 1" wide cluster of white mini blossoms and two 1¾"
    wide leaves
2 stems of dark green silk feather grass, each with three 10"
    branches of 8–10 grass sprigs
1 stem of burgundy/black silk skimmia with three 5"–11"
    sprigs of 1½"–2" long berry clusters and 2" long leaves
2 stems of burgundy silk grain, each with 5 branches of 3"
    long sprigs of many ¼" long buds
1 oz. of dark green dried isolepsis
1 oz. of light green/gray forest coral moss
3"x4"x4" block of floral foam for silks
U-shaped floral pins
low temperature glue gun and sticks

1 Cut the binding vine or wires off the wreath and discard. Pull the wreath apart at the center bottom to make it 6"–7" thick. Trim the foam to fit the pot; glue in place. Cover the foam with moss, securing with U-pins. Glue the pot into the wreath bottom.

2 Cut the upper 12" off the spirea and insert into the pot to extend up the left side of the wreath. Cut the rest of the stem into an 8" and two 7" sprigs. Insert the 8" sprig into the front of the foam, curving over the rim and down to the right. Insert the two 7" sprigs into the foam between the first two sprigs.

3 Cut the smallest skimmia sprig to 5" and the others to 12" and 9". Insert the 12" sprig at the back extending upward to the right of the 12" spirea sprig and the 9" sprig to the left of it. Insert the 5" skimmia sprig in front of the 12" spirea sprig. Cut one feather grass stem into a 14", a 10" and a 9" sprig. Insert the 14" sprig behind the 12" skimmia, the 10" sprig behind the 9" skimmia and the 9" sprig behind the 5" skimmia. Cut two 8" sprigs off the last feather grass stem; cut the last branch into two 5" sprigs. Insert an 8" grass sprig extending upward in the left side of the pot and one into the right. Insert the two 5" sprigs in the front, extending forward.

4 Cut the top of one grain stem to 9" and the rest of it to 15". Insert the 15" stem behind the 12" skimmia and the 9" stem into the left side of the pot. Cut the last grain stem into a 7" double-cluster stem and three 5"–6" single-cluster sprigs. Insert the 7" stem behind the 5" skimmia sprig and the rest evenly spaced around the front of the pot. Cut each isolepsis stem and wire to a wood pick, making them 6"–15" long. Insert them evenly spaced near materials of similar lengths. Glue eight to ten 1" moss tufts along the wreath front.

Bird & Nest

8" round twig wreath
4" rattan bird nest
4" long red feathered fat robin
two 1" long speckled plastic eggs
five 12" long cinnamon sticks
1 stem of green vinyl fir with twelve 5" sprigs, two 1½" long cones and one 3" long cone
1 stem of artificial blackberries with 3 sprigs of seven ⅜" wide berries and leaves
4 green flocked holly picks, each with 5 sprigs of three 2" long leaves and 3 red berries
1 stem of dried bell reed with at least 25 seed pods
½ oz. of reindeer moss
30-gauge wire
low temperature glue gun and sticks

1 Hold the cinnamon sticks in a bundle, offsetting them from one other, and wire in the center. Glue the bundle over the wreath near the inside back edge. Glue the nest as shown, with the bird on the sticks and the eggs in the nest.

2 Cut the cones off the fir stem and set aside. Cut the stem into a 6-sprig branch and two 3-sprig branches. Glue the 6-sprig branch behind the bird, extending upward; bend one sprig over the sticks left of the bird. Glue a 3-sprig branch right of the nest and one in front of the sticks on the left side of the wreath. Glue the large cone right of the bird, a small cone into the nest and one outside the wreath at the lower left.

3 Cut the berry stem into a 6", a 9" and a 15" sprig. Insert the 15" sprig into the left back of the wreath between the cinnamon sticks, arching it over the bird and nest. Insert the 9" sprig beside it, curving the same direction. Glue the 6" sprig along the left wreath extending forward.

4 Cut the stem of one holly pick to 1"; insert behind the 6-sprig pine branch. Cut the remaining picks into 3-leaf sprigs. Glue three around the back of the wreath, one into the nest, one near the lower left cone and the rest evenly spaced among the pine sprigs and to cover any visible glue. Cut the bell reed into 2½"–9" sprigs and glue evenly spaced near materials of similar lengths. Glue moss tufts into the nest and evenly spaced through the design.

Rose Wreath

2 yards of ⅝" wide pink wire-edged ribbon

2 stems of pink silk roses, each with a 13" section of nine 1"–1¾" wide blossoms and many leaves

1 stem of artificial blackberries with an 11" section of ⅜" wide berries and many leaves

1 stem of blue silk mini daisies with 7 sprigs of three ½" wide blossoms and 1 leaf

1 oz. of dried rice grass

six 36" strands of raffia

30-gauge wire

low temperature glue gun and sticks

1 Cut the rose stems to 18" and gently curve each into a half circle. Overlap the stems 3" and wire together (this will be the wreath top). Twist the two bottom leaves together to complete the round shape. Bend back the lowest sprig on each stem to cover the bare stems.

2 Cut the lowest berry sprig to 7". Wire it to extend left from the wreath top. Cut the rest of the berry stem to 13". Wire it to the wreath top extending right, then shape it to curve inside the wreath, making a smaller wreath.

3 Hold two raffia strands over the ribbon and handle as one to make an oblong bow (see page 26) with four

3"–3½" loops, a 10" tail, a 15" tail and a 21" tail (add raffia strands as needed). Glue it to the wreath top; wrap the 10" tail spiral fashion around the inner wreath. Wrap the 15" tail down the left side of the outer wreath and the 21" tail down the right side. Wrap the raffia tails around the outer wreath on both sides.

4 Cut the daisy stem into seven 3-flower sprigs. Glue evenly spaced among the roses, hiding their stems among the leaves. Cut the rice grass into 3"–4" sprigs. Glue in clusters evenly spaced among the roses and berries and around the bow. Attach a wire loop hanger (see page 18) to the upper back.

Harvest Arch

24" wide twig arch
8" round grapevine wreath
1 oz. of dried wild avena
six 36" strands of raffia
24-gauge wire
low temperature glue gun and sticks
3 yards of 1½" wide bronze wire-edged ribbon
2 stems of silk hazelnuts, each with a 12" and a 16" sprig of leaves and 1" wide nuts
3 stems of yellow silk sunflowers, each with a 4" wide blossom and three 4"–5" long leaves
3 stems of rust silk larkspur, each with a 12" section of many ¾"–1" wide blossoms

1 Cut the binding wires on the wreath and separate it into two equal bundles (only one will be used). Wire the wreath to the arch slightly left of the center.

2 Cut a hazelnut stem to 27". Wire it to the right side to extend 4" past the lowest twig ends, curving to follow the line of the arch. Bend the shorter sprig on this stem to curve over the right side of the wreath. Cut the other hazelnut stem into a 12" and an 18" sprig. Wire both to extend downward over the left side of the arch with the long one over the twig ends.

3 Cut one sunflower stem to 9" and two to 14". Wire a 14" stem to each side of the arch, then wire the 9" stem over the right side. Cut each larkspur stem to 15". Wire one among the flowers and nuts on each side of the arch. Wire the third stem to the wreath, curving over the right side.

4 Hold the raffia over the ribbon and handle together to make a puffy bow (see page 26) with a center loop, ten 3½" loops, a 9", a 10" and a 12" tail. Glue the bow to the arch top slightly left of the center. Cut the avena into 8"–12" sprigs and glue evenly spaced among all the flowers at similar angles. Attach a wire loop hanger (see page 18) to the back—you may have to experiment to find the balance point so the arch hangs as shown in the large photo.

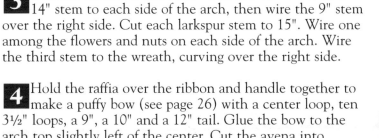

Wreath in a Wreath

16" round lacquered vine wreath
6–10 strands of raffia, 40"–48" long
1 branch of green/brown latex nuts and grape
 leaves with 3 curling sprigs, eighteen
 1½"–3½" wide leaves and 5 clusters of
 many ⅝"–¾" long nuts
3 stems of rust silk chrysanthemums, each
 with a 2" and a 3" wide blossom and 8
 leaves
3 stems of peach silk vervain, each with three
 8"–9" sprigs of feathery flowers and 3–6
 leaves
2 oz. of dried broom bloom
2 oz. of burgundy dried oak leaves
30-gauge wire
low temperature glue gun and sticks

1 Cut six fine, curling twigs from the back of the wreath and set aside for step 4. Shred two raffia strands into 5–6 very fine strands and tie together at one end. Glue the knot to the upper back of the wreath at 11:00, then wrap the ends spiral fashion around the wreath. Glue the ends at the back, then continue with another strand set, ending at 11:00.

2 Cut the lowest nut sprig with three leaves off the main stem and set aside. Wire the rest of the branch to curve over the top of the wreath and down the right side, placing the lowest leaves at 11:00. Tie five raffia strands together at one end, then shred each into 5–6 fine strands. Form into a 9" wide circle with a 20" tail; tie with a short strand to secure. Glue this new "wreath" to the vine wreath slightly left of the center top, angled over the left side. Glue the reserved nut sprig and leaves extending from 11:00 downward to the left.

3 Cut two mum stems to 13". Wire one to the vine wreath, curving and extending right to the end of the nut stem. Wire the second to extend right from 11:00 on the vine wreath. Cut the last mum stem into two 5" sprigs. Glue both extending left from 11:00 with the large blossom closer to the center top. Cut each vervain stem into three 8" sprigs. Glue two extending from 11:00 left and one curving downward and left over the right side of the raffia wreath. Glue the rest evenly spaced over the right side of the vine wreath.

4 Cut the oak leaves off the stems and glue evenly spaced, extending outward and toward the wreath edges. Cut the broom bloom into 4"–5" sprigs and glue evenly spaced among all the materials with some around the outer edge of the wreath. Glue the twigs from step one evenly spaced throughout the design as shown in the large photo. Add a wire loop hanger (see page 18) to the top back.

Daisies on a Heart

13" wide vine heart with a 24" tail
2½ yards of 1½" wide moss green taffeta wire-edged
ribbon
2 stems of white artificial wild daisies, each with three
13" sprigs of many ¾" wide blossoms and leaves
1 stem of yellow artificial wild daisies with three 13"
sprigs of many ¾" wide blossoms and leaves
2 stems of silk blackberries, each with two 9" sprigs of
twelve ⅝" wide berries and wired leaves
4 oz. of dark green preserved wild boxwood
24-gauge wire
low temperature glue gun and sticks

1 Cut each white daisy stem into three 13"
sprigs. Glue three to extend from the heart
bottom up the left side and over the left shoulder.
Glue the other three to extend 15" down from the
center bottom.

2 Cut each berry stem into two 9" sprigs, each
with 11–12 berries. Glue two extending up
the left side of the heart and over the shoulder.
Glue the other two extending downward among
the white daisies to 13" below the heart bottom.

3 Cut the yellow daisy stem into nine 4½"–5½"
sprigs. Glue four evenly spaced extending
upward among the other materials and five
extending downward.

4 Use the ribbon to make an oblong bow (see
page 26) with a center loop, eight 2"–3½"
loops, a 13" and a 15" tail. Glue to the heart center bottom. Tuck and glue the short tail up the left
side and the 15" tail among the materials which
extend below the heart. Cut the boxwood into
5"–7" sprigs. Glue them evenly spaced among all
the previous materials at similar angles. Glue 3"
boxwood sprigs and any remaining 3" daisy sprigs
above and below the bow center. Attach a wire
loop hanger (see page 18) to the back.

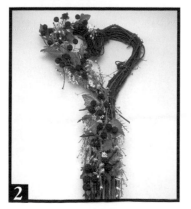

INDEX

(Bold print indicates project title.)